Schottenfreude

Also by BEN SCHOTT

Schott's Original Miscellany

Schott's Food & Drink Miscellany

Schott's Sporting, Gaming, & Idling Miscellany

Schott's Almanac (2006–2011)

Schott's Quintessential Miscellany

Schottenfreude

GERMAN WORDS FOR THE HUMAN CONDITION

Conceived, written, & designed by

BEN SCHOTT

mit Wortschatzunterstützung von

Dr Oscar Bandtlow

JOHN MURRAY

KEY TO THE ENTRIES

#

𝕲erman 𝕸ord

approximate phonetic pronunciation (with stresses underlined)

English translation of the German word's meaning.

GERMAN-WORD-COMPOUND-CONSTRUCTION

Cross-references to related words are marked: ☜ ☟ ☞

The few German words that have no explanatory note are marked: {✖}

The hierarchy of footnotes within each explanatory note is: † ‡ * § ‡ ∴ ⁞ ⊛ ⌑ △ ◇

Footnotes that do not directly relate to text in the note above are marked: »

Footnotes relating to the German word, or its translation, are marked: ☞

URLs within footnotes have been shortened using *bit.ly* addresses.

"The German language is sufficiently copious and productive,
to furnish native words for any idea that can be expressed at all."

Charles Follen, *A Practical Grammar of the German Language* (Hilliard, Gray, 1835), 170

1   "Kicking leaves, sand, pebbles, etc." is listed as #174 on the "Pleasant Events Schedule" – "a self-report behavioural inventory of the frequency of occurrence and subjective enjoyability of a number of commonly rewarding events," devised in 1972 by the psychologists D. J. MacPhillamy and P. M. Lewinsohn.[†] Other events on this 320-item schedule include:

#18   Going naked
#26   Breathing clean air
#185   Feeling the presence of the Lord in my life

† D. J. MacPhillamy & P. M. Lewinsohn, "The Pleasant Events Schedule," *Journal of Consulting and Clinical Psychology* 50, № 3 (Jun 1982): 363–80.
» The life-affirming quality of this action is given additional poignancy by the association of autumnal leaves with human souls – made by a pantheon of poets including Virgil (*Aeneid*, VI, ll. 309–12); Dante (*Inferno*, III, ll. 112–14); Percy Bysshe Shelley ("Ode to the West Wind"); and John Milton: "Angel forms, who lay intranc'd / Thick as autumnal leaves that strow the brooks / In Vallombrosa" (*Paradise Lost*, I, ll. 301–03). See John Conington's commentary, *The Works of Virgil* (George Bell, 1884), vol. 2, 467.

2   For the deliciously pernickety Noël Coward, a surprising number of people personified the perfect houseguest, including: John Gielgud, because he was "amusing, talkative and most considerate"; Rebecca West, who – despite tribulations with her gallbladder – was "gay and considerate and, oh, how gloriously intelligent"; and Hester Chapman, who was "perfectly happy to be left alone with a book and not demanding to be entertained";[†] Natasha Wilson, too, because "she never spoke to anyone before luncheon."[‡]

† *The Noël Coward Diaries*, eds. Graham Payn & Sheridan Morley (1982) (Da Capo Press, 2000), 249, 515, 648.
‡ Philip Hoare, *Noël Coward: A Biography* (1995) (University of Chicago Press, 1998), 408.
» Coward was, of course, no slouch as houseguest himself. One of the properties he visited (although as a renter) was Ian Fleming's Jamaican retreat, Goldeneye. After his stay, Coward penned a (slightly barbed and not particularly good) thank-you poem, titled "House Guest." See *The Letters of Noël Coward*, ed. Barry Day (Alfred A. Knopf, 2007), 540–41.

3   This odour is a combination of the volatile organic compounds (VOCs) found in car surfaces, adhesives, and sealants, the most dominant of which (in order of their concentration) are: "toluene, acetone/pentane, o-xylene/styrene, 1,2,4-trimethylbenzene, m,p-xylene, various C_{7-12} alkanes, ethylbenzene, n-hexane, and ethylene glycol butyl ether."[†]

In the *West Wing* episode "18th and Potomac,"[‡] President Josiah Bartlet tells his secretary, Dolores Landingham, that the interior smell of her brand-new car is "the smell of freedom" – shortly after which she is killed in a collision with a drunk driver.

† Stephen K. Brown & Min Chen, "Volatile Organic Compounds (VOCs) in New Car Interiors," paper presented at the 15th International Clean Air & Environment Conference, Sydney, 26–30 xi 2000.
‡ Aaron Sorkin, "18th and Potomac," *The West Wing*, 2001.

1

Herbstlaubtrittvergnügen

hairbst-laowb – tritt-fair-gnuu-ghen

Kicking through piles of autumn leaves.

AUTUMN-FOLIAGE-STRIKE-FUN

2

Gastdruck

gahst – drook

The exhausting effort of being a good houseguest.

GUEST-PRESSURE

3

Kraftfahrzeugsinnenausstattungsneugeruchsgenuss

krahft-fahr-tsoygs – in-nen-aows-staht-toongs – noy-ghe-rooochs – ghe-noose

New car smell.

AUTOMOBILE-INTERIOR-FURNISHING-NEW-AROMA-PLEASURE

Schattenfreude

4 V. S. Naipaul perfectly described the clarity of new spectacles, in a letter to his mother, written while he was a student at University College, Oxford:

> The world seemed such a glorious place. I could see people much clearer; and streets became more beautiful. The colours are sharper for me. And I feel rather sorry to have missed all those wonderful colours all this time.[†]

Zadie Smith gave an equally sharp-eyed account:

> The first day she wore glasses had been a little like this: lines sharper, colours clearer. The whole world like an old painting restored.[‡]

[†] Letter dated 3 x 1952; V. S. Naipaul, *Between Father and Son: Family Letters* (Alfred A. Knopf, 1999), 201.

[‡] Zadie Smith, *On Beauty* (Penguin, 2005), eBook.

5 Both Mark Twain and Arthur Conan Doyle are reputed to have sent telegrams to friends and prominent men (respectively) that read something akin to:

ALL IS DISCOVERED, FLEE AT ONCE*!*

These midlarious japes enjoyed varying degrees of success, depending on which unlikely source you believe.

» Discussing "vital" and "mechanical" movements, Bertrand Russell noted, "It requires only a very slight expenditure of energy to send a post-card with the words 'All is discovered; fly!' but the effect in generating kinetic energy is said to be amazing." *The Analysis of Mind* (George Allen & Unwin, 1921), 48.

» P. G. Wodehouse memorably described a character as looking "like an American Senator who has received an anonymous telegram saying, 'All is discovered. Fly at once.'" *Money for Nothing* (1928) (Barrie & Jenkins, 1976), 212.

» Robert Penn Warren wrote of the "West": "It is where you go when you get the letter saying: *Flee, all is discovered*. It is where you go when you look down at the blade in your hand and the blood on it." *All the King's Men* (1946) (Harvest, 1996), 405–06.

» See also Edward Gorey, "The Admonitory Hippopotamus: or, Angelica and Sneezby," in *Amphigorey Again* (Harvest, 2007).

6 It would be foolish to discuss thirst without turning to Professor James T. Fitzsimons, who wrote:

> The gratification of thirst is universally held to be one of the pleasures of life; the sensation cannot be ignored, and if water be lacking, thirst comes to dominate our thoughts and behaviour; it drives us to the utmost endeavour and achievement … or to the depths of despair and degradation.[†]

Samuel Taylor Coleridge vividly described this despair:

> With throats unslaked, with black lips baked,
> We could nor laugh nor wail;
> Through utter drought all dumb we stood!
> I bit my arm, I sucked the blood,
> And cried, A sail! a sail![‡]

[†] James T. Fitzsimons, *The Physiology of Thirst and Sodium Appetite* (Cambridge University Press, 1979), 1.

[‡] Samuel Taylor Coleridge, *The Rime of the Ancient Mariner* (1798), pt III, ll. 157–61.

4

Brillenbrillanz

brihl-len – brihl-lahnts

~

The sudden, innervating clarity afforded by new glasses.

SPECTACLES-LUMINOSITY

5

Schuldaufdeckungsangst

shoold – aowf-deh-koongs – ahngst

~

The fear that you will be found out.

GUILT-EXPOSURE-ANXIETY

6

Tantalusqualerlösung

tahn-tah-loose-kvahl – ehr-loo-zoong

~

The relief and delight of perfectly slaked thirst.

TANTALUS-TORMENT-REDEMPTION

Schattenfreude

7 Jerome K. Jerome wrote: "I never could read my own handwriting. There is only one man who can, and he lives with me, and I have insured his life for several thousands of pounds."[†] Jerome may have been joking, but Tolstoy relied heavily on his wife, as his son wrote:

Sometimes, when anything was written quite illegibly, she would go to my father's study and ask him what it meant. … My father would take the manuscript in his hand, ask with some annoyance: "What on earth is the difficulty?" and begin to read it out loud. When he came to the difficult place he would mumble and hesitate, and sometimes had the greatest difficulty in making out, or rather in guessing, what he had written.[‡]

[†] *The Idler*, vol. 5 (Chatto & Windus, 1894), 326.
[‡] Ilya Tolstoy, *Reminiscences of [Leo] Tolstoy*, trans. George Calderon (Century, 1914), 137–38.
➜ Ludwig van Beethoven once wrote, "My handwriting is misunderstood as often as I am myself." Lewis Lockwood, *Beethoven: The Music and the Life* (W. W. Norton, 2005), 493.

8 This portmanteau-portmanteau describes a range of pleasing acts of quotidian legerdemain, including:

Locating and unpicking a frayed end of tape. ❦ Tightening a minuscule screw. ❦ Shuffling cards. ❦ Unhooking a bra. ❦ Sliding your queen across a chessboard. ❦ Spinning a coin. ❦ Chalking a cue. ❦ Knotting a (bow) tie. ❦ Removing a recalcitrant sticker in one unbroken peel. ❦ Fingertipping something off a high shelf. ❦ Locating a tiny reset button. ❦ (Dis)proving WET PAINT signs. (☞ 55) ❦ Unknotting. ❦ Changing a cartridge without inking your fingers. ❦ Fastening a bracelet. ❦ Testing for dust by gliding your finger along a surface. ❦ Twisting wire ties. ❦ Flicking the bean. ❦ Counting money. ❦ Riffling casino chips. ❦ Stroking a corrugated surface. ❦ Jenga dislodgement. ❦ Moustache twirling. ❦ Rolling a joint. ❦ Jetting a hosepipe with your thumb. ❦ Hopping a Halma pawn. ❦ Plucking a chocolate from a selection box. ❦ Tapping for cavities. ❦ Opening Tetra Paks. ❦ Disentangling. ❦ Kinking a metal tape measure into a corner. (☞ 68) ❦ Identifying an object by touch. ❦ Tumbling a safe. ❦ Inserting a USB plug right-side up, first time. ❦ Jiggling on your fingertips, say, half a toasted bagel while transferring it to a plate.

9 As E. V. Lucas noted, "Nothing can deprive the secret passage of its glamour; not all the Tubes, or subways, or river tunnelling, through which we pass so naturally day after day. … Just as an ordinary desk takes on a new character directly one is told that it has a secret drawer, so does even a whisper of a secret passage transfigure the most commonplace house."[†]

Edward Bulwer-Lytton – coiner of the phrase "It was a dark and stormy night" – wrote: "How could I help writing romances after living amongst the secret panels and hiding-places of our dear old home? How often have I trembled with fear at the sound of my own footsteps when I ventured into the picture gallery! How fearfully have I glanced at the faces of my ancestors as I peered into the shadowy abysses of the 'secret chamber.' It was years before I could venture inside without my hair literally bristling with terror."[‡]

[†] Edward Verrall Lucas, *Adventures and Enthusiasms* (George H. Doran, 1920), 244–46.
[‡] Quoted in Allan Fea, *Secret Chambers and Hiding-Places* (1901) (Methuen, 1908), 14.

7

Ludwigssyndrom

lood-vigs – zoon-drohm

Discovering an indecipherable note in your own handwriting.

LUDWIG'S-SYNDROME

8

Fingerspitzentanz

fing-er-shpits-en – tahnts

Tiny triumphs of nimble-fingered dexterity.

FINGERTIPS-DANCE

9

Geheimgangsverlockung

ghe-hime-gahngs – fair-lok-koong

The conviction that all old, large houses must contain secret passages.

SECRET-CORRIDOR-SEDUCTION

Schottenfreude

10 The physician M. L. Este rather recklessly advised:

> Water is never to be entered gradually by *inches*, for the sensation, then, is unpleasant. A beginner, who always has some aversion to the element, should muster resolution and throw himself in; for the same reason that any disagreeable medicine is not to be taken sip by sip.[†]

While diving into cold water is decisive, it is agreed that gradual entry mitigates a range of risks, from transient global amnesia and cold stimulus headache to cardiac arrest. Dr Gordon Giesbrecht advises a "1–10–1" approach to survive ice-water immersion: control your breathing in the first minute of panic; use the next ten minutes to plan an escape; and you then have an hour before you are incapacitated by hypothermia.[‡]

[†] M. L. Este, *Remarks on Baths* (Gale, Curtis, & Fenner, 1812), 69.

[‡] See G. G. Giesbrecht & J. A. Wilkerson, *Hypothermia, Frostbite, and Other Cold Injuries* (Mountaineers Books, 2006), 62.

» A traditional remedy for nosebleeds was to pour ice-cold water over the genitals (which would, at the very least, be distracting).

---

11 Induced motion, as this phenomenon is known, was explored by the psychologist Karl Duncker, who placed subjects in a dark room and projected a dot of light enclosed in a larger frame of light. When the frame was moved from side to side, the subjects perceived the dot to move in the opposite direction.[†] ❦ An appreciation of induced motion goes back to Euclid of Alexandria (the "Father of Geometry"), who discussed the sensation in his treatise *Optics* (*c.*300 B.C.):[‡]

If, when certain objects are moved, one is obviously not moved, the object that is not moved will appear to move backward. For, let B and D move, and let G remain unmoved, and from the eye let the rays fall, ZB, ZG, and ZD. So B, as it moves, will be nearer to G, and D, receding, will be farther away; therefore G will seem to move in the opposite direction.

[†] Karl Duncker, "Über induzierte Bewegung," *Psychologische Forschung* 12, № 1 (1929): 180–259.

[‡] "The Optics of Euclid," trans. H. E. Burton, *Journal of the Optical Society of America* 35, № 5 (May 1945): 371.

---

12 This universal pleasure was iconically captured by Oscar Hammerstein II, who ranked it fifth in his catalogue of 14 "favorite things." That said, some cultures are more preoccupied with wrapping than others. Japan's highly intricate tradition of gift-giving has evolved an equally labyrinthine etiquette of wrapping. To take just one small detail: the traditional cord used to wrap gifts – *mizuhiki* (水引) – is employed in a variety of symbolic colour combinations, for example:

Weddings .... GOLD & SILVER
Condolences .... WHITE; BLACK; SILVER; BLUE; &c.
Felicitous occasions .... RED & WHITE; RED & GOLD

When colours are paired, convention dictates placement (e.g., red *mizuhiki* is always to the right of white). And since odd numbers are lucky, *mizuhiki* are sold in uneven sets, though wedding gifts are often wrapped with two sets of five-strand *mizuhiki*, since ten is considered an auspicious number.

» See, for example, Kunio Ekiguchi, *Gift Wrapping: Creative Ideas from Japan* (Kodansha America, 1985).

10

Intimbereichsverkrampfung

in-teem – beh-rikes – fair-krahm-pfoong

~

Reluctance to enter cold water, felt progressively at each erogenous zone.

GENITAL-AREA-CLENCHING

11

Eisenbahnscheinbewegung

eye-zen-bahn – shine-beh-veh-goong

~

The false sensation of movement when, looking out from a stationary train, you see another train depart.

RAILWAY-ILLUSION-MOTION

12

Wohlverpackungsfreude

vole – fair-pah-koongs – froy-duh

~

The uncomplicated delight of a perfectly wrapped parcel.

WELL-WRAPPING-PLEASURE

Schadenfreude

13 Walking is often a catalyst to thought. Jean-Jacques Rousseau observed, "I can scarcely think when I remain still; my body must be in motion to make my mind active."[†] Søren Kierkegaard said, "I have walked myself into my best thoughts."[‡] And Johann Wolfgang von Goethe wrote, "That which I find the best in contemplation, thoughts, even expression comes to me most often while walking. While sitting I am in the mood for nothing."[*] When a visitor asked to see William Wordsworth's study, the poet's maid replied, "Here is his library, but his study is out of doors."[§] According to the celebrated German poet Heinrich Heine:

> The neighbours knew that it was exactly half-past three o'clock when Immanuel Kant stepped forth from his house in his grey, tight-fitting coat, with his Spanish cane in his hand, and betook himself to the little linden avenue called after him to this day the "Philosopher's Walk."[ː]

Napoleon Bonaparte sometimes dictated as he walked, as did William McKinley, G.K. Chesterton, Irving Berlin, Winston Churchill, Joseph Stalin, and others.

For Bertrand Russell, "our mental make-up is suited to a life of very severe physical labour,"[∴] and he often trudged along on walking tours to prove it. Arthur Schopenhauer preferred to pace the streets alone, startling passers-by with his muttered thoughts; he wrote:

> The pen is to thought what the stick is to walking, but one walks most easily without a stick, and thinks most perfectly when no pen is at hand.[ː]

Sherlock Holmes, however, preferred the great indoors:

> "It is quite a three-pipe problem, and I beg that you won't speak to me for fifty minutes." He curled himself up in his chair, with his thin knees drawn up to his hawk-like nose, and there he sat with his eyes closed.[⊛]

Friedrich Nietzsche quoted Gustave Flaubert as saying, "One cannot think and write except when seated" – before damning the sentiment as a nihilist sin against the Holy Ghost. "Only thoughts *won by walking* are valuable," Nietzsche wrote in *The Twilight of the Idols*.[ᴴ]

† *Confessions of Jean-Jacques Rousseau* (Oliver & Boyd, 1904), 166.

‡ From an 1847 letter to his niece. Roger Poole, *Kierkegaard: The Indirect Communication* (University Press of Virginia, 1993), 172.

* Journal entry, 21 iii 1780, quoted in Katharina Mommsen, *Goethe's Art of Living* (Trafford, 2003), 69.

§ As recounted by Henry David Thoreau in "Walking," *The Atlantic Monthly* 9, № 56 (Jun 1862): 657–74. Thoreau added, "You must walk like a camel, which is said to be the only beast which ruminates when walking."

ː Heinrich Heine, *Religion and Philosophy in Germany: A Fragment*, trans. John Snodgrass (Trübner, 1882), 108.

∴ Bertrand Russell, "What Desires Are Politically Important?" (Nobel lecture), in *The Basic Writings* (Routledge, 2009), 451.

ː *Essays of Schopenhauer*, trans. Mrs Rudolf Dircks (Walter Scott, 1897), 10. Schopenhauer told the story of an Austrian who said: "You like walking alone; so do I: therefore we can go together."

⊛ Arthur Conan Doyle, "The Red-Headed League," *The Strand Magazine* 2 (Jul–Dec 1891): 197. (It is therefore ironic that London is now thick with Sherlock Holmes walking tours.)

ᴴ *The Works of Friedrich Nietzsche*, vol. xi, ed. Alexander Tille, trans. Thomas Common (Macmillan, 1896), 102. Here Flaubert is quoted as declaring: *"On ne peut penser et écrire qu'assis."*

↝ *Erkenntnis* also means "insight," "knowledge," "realization," &c.; *Spaziergang* is on friendly terms with the Italian *passeggiata*.

13

Erkenntnisspaziergang

air-kent-niss – shpah-tseer-gahng

~

A perambulation taken with the specific intention of contemplation.

COGNITION-STROLL

14
{✕}

Deppenfahrerbeäugung

dep-pen-fahr-er – beh-oy-goong

~

The urge to turn and glare at a bad driver you've just overtaken.

MORON-DRIVER-EYEBALLING

15
{✕}

Saukopfsülzensehnsucht

zow-kohpf – zuul-tsen – zehn-zooccht

~

A shameful love of bad food.

PIG'S-HEAD-ASPIC-DESIRE

16 "The matter from which that absent stair is made constitutes matter itself"† – according to the French writer and "'pataphysicist" Jean Ferry.‡

† Quoted in André Breton, ed., *Anthology of Black Humor*, trans. Mark Polizzotti (City Lights Books, 1997), 329.
‡ The *nom d'emprunt* of Jean-André Lévy.
» Nicholson Baker likened the effect of such "disruptions of physical routines" to riding a "curve of incredulousness and resignation." *The Mezzanine* (1988) (Granta Books, 1990), 13. P. G. Wodehouse described the effect as a "sick shock." *The Adventures of Sally* (1922) (Penguin, 1986), 16.
» In 1903, T. W. Connor wrote a music hall song recounting how nine men died on their first day at work. The fourth verse described the death of "Jerry Macintyre" – who "went to do a moving job":

> With a grand piano on his back,
> Upstairs he tried to run,
> Trod on a stair that wasn't there, –
> And his day's work was done!*

* T. W. Connor, "And His Day's Work Was Done," sixpenny popular edition, sung by George Brooks (Francis, Day, & Hunter, 1903).

17 This sensation was memorably described by the French film theorist Christian Metz:

> Spectators, on leaving, brutally expelled from the black interior of the cinema into the vivid and unkind light of the lobby, sometimes have the bewildered face … of people just waking up. Leaving the cinema is a bit like getting out of bed: not always easy.†

Italo Calvino wrote of the (equally unsettling) opposite experience: "I had gone in in broad daylight, and came out to find it dark, the lamp-lit streets prolonging the black-and-white of the screen."‡

† Quoted in Victor Burgin, *The Remembered Film* (Reaktion Books, 2004), 30.
‡ Quoted in Gabriele Pedullà, *In Broad Daylight: Movies and Spectators After the Cinema* (2008) (Verso, 2012), eBook.
» Lighting engineers call this phenomenon "adaptation glare," and it similarly affects drivers who exit long road tunnels into daylight. See, for example, B. Wördenweber et al., *Automotive Lighting and Human Vision* (Springer, 2007), 274.

18 In her tautologically titled memoir, the Duchess of York advised her readers to "watch 'FOMO' – Fear Of Missing Out" – and warned: "This will make you go down wrong paths."† Immanuel Kant made this related observation on how different character temperaments behave in society:

> The sanguineous person goes where he is not invited; the choleric one does not go where he is not invited in accordance with propriety; the melancholic one ~~doesn't come at all~~ prevents [himself from] not being invited at all.‡

† Sarah Ferguson, the Duchess of York, *Finding Sarah: A Duchess's Journey to Find Herself* (Simon & Schuster, 2011), 106.
‡ Immanuel Kant, *Observations on the Feeling of the Beautiful and Sublime and Other Writings*, eds. Patrick Frierson & Paul Guyer (Cambridge University Press, 2011), 114.
» Outside the sphere of social engagements, a devastating form of FOMO comes with the "scarcity psychology" of panic buying and hoarding food, which "operates like a run on a bank; a contagion where every step and every noise accelerates the effect." Mark Edwards, *Biowar 1* (TalentDNA Press, 2008), 186.

16

Leertretung

lair – treh-toong

~

Stepping down heavily on a stair that isn't there.

VOID-STEPPING

17

Tageslichtspielschock

tah-ghess – liccht-shpeel – shok

~

Being startled when exiting a cinema into broad daylight.

DAY-LIGHT-SHOW-SHOCK

18

Ausbremsungsangst

aowss-brem-zoongs – ahngst

~

Fear of missing out (on a social event).

THWARTING-FEAR

Schottenfreude

19 & 20 The ability to recall the location of material within books, as well as the shelving whereabouts of specific books, was the subject of correspondence to *Nature*, in 1880. The following is from a letter written by the British insurance expert Cornelius Walford:

> I have a very large and still increasing library, but there is hardly a volume, or indeed a tract, the appearance and condition of which does not at once present itself to my mind if occasion to use it should arise. Further, being engaged in the compilation of a work some years since, wherein many references to other books were necessary, I used, when away from home (as was frequently the case) to write and indicate not simply in what part of the library the book would be found, but in what portion of the volume, and almost always whether on the left or right hand page, any given passage required would be found.[†]

---

† Cornelius Walford, letter to the editor, *Nature* 22 (8 vii 1880): 220–21.

21 The Slovenian thinker Slavoj Žižek described the effect of the "accidentally produced 'little piece of the real'" encountered in horoscopes and fortune-telling:

> A totally contingent coincidence is sufficient for the effect of transference to take place; we become convinced that "there is something to it."[†]

Carl Gustav Jung touched on this subject in his statistical analysis of marriage, horoscopes, and synchronicity:

> I know, however, from long experience of these things that spontaneous synchronistic phenomena draw the observer, by hook or by crook, into what is happening and occasionally make him an accessory to the deed.[‡]

In his 1950s analysis of horoscopes, Theodor Adorno hilariously dissected the techniques and tropes of the newspaper astrologer. (He noted, for example, how the "contradictory requirements of life" were conveniently solved by predicting hard work in the morning and pleasure later in the day.) Yet Adorno's conclusion was more serious. Arguing that Adolf Hitler rose to power partly because "people never quite fully believe what they pretend to believe," Adorno suggested that "astrology has to be regarded as a little model of much greater social feeding on paranoid dispositions."[*] He ended by invoking Gottfried Leibniz, who wrote in 1714: "I despise almost nothing, except judicial [fortune-telling] astrology and trickeries of that kind."[§]

---

† Slavoj Žižek, *Looking Awry: An Introduction to Jacques Lacan Through Popular Culture* (1991) (MIT Press, 1992), 31.
‡ Carl Gustav Jung, *Synchronicity* (Princeton University Press, 2010), 63.
* Theodor W. Adorno, "The Stars Down to Earth," *Telos* 19 (Spring 1974): 13–90. Adorno performed a content analysis of Carroll Righter's daily "Astrological Forecasts" column in the *Los Angeles Times* between November 1952 and February 1953.
§ Gottfried Leibniz, *The Monadology and Other Philosophical Writings*, trans. Robert Latta (Clarendon Press, 1898), 154.
» Kelvin MacKenzie, when editor of *The Sun*, is said to have sacked the paper's astrologer with a letter that began, "As you will already know …" See Piers Morgan, *The Insider* (Ebury Press, 2005), 277.
➤ *Zwillingsmoral* combines *Zwillinge* ("twins" and the Zodiac sign Gemini) with *Doppelmoral* ("double standard").

Schlüsselszenenadlerauge

shluu-sel-stseh-nen – ahd-ler-ow-ghe

Knowing from memory where a specific passage is located in a book.

KEY-SCENE-EAGLE-EYE

Buchadlerauge

boocch – ahd-ler-ow-ghe

Knowing from memory where a specific book may be found on a shelf.

BOOK-EAGLE-EYE

Zwillingsmoral

tsvill-ings – moh-rahl

Reading horoscopes you don't believe in.

GEMINI-STANDARD

Schottenfreude

22 This portmanteau-portmanteau describes some of the zeniths and nadirs of friendship:

The friend whose mere name prompts a smile. ❦ Relief when a friend marries someone you like. ❦ The friend who remembers everything you've ever said or done.[†] ❦ Hoping that a friend's success will somehow profit you. ❦ Friends with benefits.[‡] ❦ When too much water has flowed to revivify a friendship. ❦ Rekindling a friendship to see whether it is still genuine. ❦ When a friend you turned to in a crisis never lets you forget.[*] ❦ When a friend you helped in a crisis never forgives you for knowing. ❦ Frenemies.[§] ❦ When friendships fade.[‡] ❦ Disliking your friend's friends. ❦ Friendship mathematics (+, −, ×, ÷) catalysed by a new romantic relationship. (☞ 71, 81) ❦ Getting high with a little help from your friends. ❦ When a friend's success plucks him or her from your orbit. ❦ BFFs.[∴] ❦ The friend who makes you feel terrible.[ː] ❦ Forgiving the foibles of friends, as they forgive yours. ❦ When even divorce seems easier than breaking up with an old friend.[⊛] ❦ Simpatico. (☞ 29) ❦ Sensing (hoping) that you will become friends with someone you've just met. ❦ Frenvy. ❦ The delight and significance of making new friends in later life.[¤] ❦

When profligacy with friendships precludes intimacy. ❦ The belief that friendship and enmity are affiliated.[△] ❦ Seeing a friend in a new context (e.g., at work). ❦ The necessity of decency in the heart of all true friends.[◇]

[†] "Forgetfulness in friendship may sometimes be as necessary as memory." Owen Felltham, *Resolves* (John Hatchard, 1806), 225.
[‡] "Basically, if it feels right and you[r] friend agrees ... do it." Labotomous Leek, *Friends with Benefits* (Funkzilla Press, 2005), 10.
[*] "In the distress of our best friends we always find something that does not displease us." François de La Rochefoucauld, *Maxims and Moral Reflections* (Edinburgh, 1775), 50–51.
[§] "Thy friendship oft has made my heart to ache: / Do be my enemy – for friendship's sake." *The Lyrical Poems of William Blake* (Clarendon Press, 1905), 164.
[‡] "Do not keep on with a mockery of friendship. ... Bury the carcase [*sic*] of friendship: it is not worth embalming." William Hazlitt, "On the Conduct of Life," *Essays* (Walter Scott, 1889), 210.
[∴] Helaine Becker asks in *The Quiz Book for BFFs*, "Are you and your pal BFFs or BFFN (Best Friends, For Now)?" (Scholastic, 2012), 4.
[ː] "You can not afford to be a friend to any one who leaves slime on you." Henry Ward Beecher, *The Original Plymouth Pulpit* (Pilgrim Press, 1897), vol. 1, 230.

[⊛] "Love is only chatter, / Friends are all that matter." Gelett Burgess, "Willy and the Lady," *A Gage of Youth* (Small, Maynard, 1907), 46.
[¤] "If a man does not make new acquaintance as he advances through life, he will soon find himself left alone." Samuel Johnson, quoted in James Boswell, *The Life of Samuel Johnson* (1791) (Jones, 1827), 80.
[△] "The qualities of your friends will be those of your enemies: cold friends, cold enemies; half friends, half enemies; fervid enemies, warm friends." J. C. Lavater, *Aphorisms* (London, 1794), 174.
[◇] "There can be no true friendship without virtue" (*Sine virtute esse amicitia nullo pacto potest*). Caius Crispus Sallust, quoted in Edwin N. Brown, *Treasury of Latin Gems* (Normal, 1894), 112.

◆　◆　◆

23 This subject is explored by William Miller in his fascinating book *The Anatomy of Disgust*: "There is no doubt that our own snot, faeces, and urine are contaminating and disgusting to us. If they weren't we would hardly be so fascinated by or curious about them."[†]

[†] William Ian Miller, *The Anatomy of Disgust* (Harvard University Press, 1997), 118.

22

☞ 71, 81

Freundschaftskalkül

froynd-shahfts – kahl-kuul

˄

The ever-changing complexity and diplomacy of friendships.

FRIENDSHIP-CALCULUS

23

☞ 30, 77

Stuhlgangsgenuss

shtool-gahngs – ghe-noose

˄

Private enjoyment of your own unsavoury bodily functions.

POO(P)LEASURE

24

{✕}

☞ 67

Luftfahrtorigaminiedergeschlagenheit

looft-fahrt – oh-ree-gah-me – nee-der-ghe-shlah-ghen-hite

˄

The sense of deflation when your diligently folded paper airplane beaks immediately to the floor.

AVIATION-ORIGAMI-DESPONDENCY

Schottenfreude

25 The psychiatrist John Oldham astutely observed:

> The unconscious conviction of one's immortality is challenged by the decline and death of one's parents. For the first time in one's life one can no longer secretly cling to the belief that it is still someone else's turn to die.[†]

Or, as the sociologist Michael Kearl put it, "One's own generation is the next to face the grim reaper and … one's own ending countdown has begun."[‡]

[†] J. Oldham, "Middle-Aged Children and Their Parents," in *The Middle Years*, eds. J. Oldham & R. Liebert (Yale University Press, 1989), 93.
[‡] Michael C. Kearl, *Endings: A Sociology of Death and Dying* (Oxford University Press, 1989), 465.
[»] The death of a parent may also bring relief (☞ 108). After his mother died, Sigmund Freud wrote of a "growth in personal freedom," in part because she would never learn of his death. See Peter Gay, *Freud: A Life for Our Time* (W. W. Norton, 1998), 573.

26

27 The great epigrammatist Martial (Marcus Valerius Martialis) urged the teachers of Rome to grant their students clemency during the heat of midsummer, and to take up their canes again only in mid-October:

> Schoolmaster, be indulgent to your simple scholars; if you would have many a long-haired youth resort to your lectures, and the class seated round your critical table love you. So may no teacher of arithmetic, or of swift writing [shorthand], be surrounded by a greater ring of pupils. The days are bright, and glow under the flaming constellation of the Lion, and fervid July is ripening the teeming harvest. Let the Scythian scourge with its formidable thongs, such as flogged [the satyr] Marsyas of Celænæ, and the terrible cane, the schoolmaster's sceptre, be laid aside, and sleep until the Ides of October. *In summer, if boys preserve their health, they do enough.*[†]

[†] Martial, *Epigrams* bk x, 62, in *The Epigrams of Martial* (Henry G. Bohn, 1860), 478; italics added.

25

☞ 53, 108

Unsterblichkeitstod

oon-shtairb-blicch-kites – tohdt

Intimations of mortality when your last surviving parent dies.

IMMORTALITY-DEATH

26

Baggerspion

bahg-gher – shpee-ohn

The urge to peek into boarded-up construction sites.

DIGGER-TRUCK-SPYHOLE

27

☞ 65

Sommerferienewigkeitsgefühl

zohm-mer-fair-ee-en – eh-vig-kites – ghe-fuul

Childhood sensation that the summer holidays will last forever.

SUMMER-VACATION-ETERNITY-FEELING

Schottenfreude

28 A number of writers have noted how familiarity breeds content, including John Webster:

> Is not old wine wholesomest, old pippins toothsomest, old wood burn brightest, old linen wash whitest? Old soldiers, sweetheart, are surest, and old lovers are soundest.[†]

And Oliver Goldsmith:

> I love everything that's old: old friends, old times, old manners, old books, old wine.[‡]

Though Desiderius Erasmus cautioned:

> The good Man does not love old Things so well, but that he had rather have his Porridge fresh than stale.[*]

[†] John Webster, *Westward Ho!*, c.1604, A II, S ii.
[‡] Oliver Goldsmith, *She Stoops to Conquer*, 1773, A I, S i.
[*] *The Colloquies of Erasmus*, trans. N. Bailey, ed. Rev. E. Johnson (Reeves & Turner, 1878), vol. I, 202.

29 "Simpatico" is notoriously tricky to translate in its full glory, though E. M. Forster came close:

> The person who understands us at first sight, who never irritates us, who never bores, to whom we can pour forth every thought and wish, not only in speech but in silence – that is what I mean by *simpatico*.[†]

The philosopher Michael Oakeshott touched on the essence of simpatico in defining "a friend":

> Somebody who engages the imagination, who excites contemplation, who provokes interest, sympathy, delight and loyalty simply on account of the relationship entered into.[‡]

[†] E. M. Forster, *Where Angels Fear to Tread* (William Blackwood, 1905), 86.
[‡] Michael Oakeshott, "On Being Conservative" (1956), in *Rationalism in Politics and Other Essays* (Methuen, 1962), 177.
➻ This rather curious word, or elements of it, were current among some German schoolchildren in the 1970s and 1980s.

30 Charles Darwin examined this tension while testing an observation by the German zoologist Alfred Brehm, that monkeys "have a great horror of everything that creeps, and especially of Snakes."[†] Darwin placed a paper bag containing a live snake on the floor of a monkey house, and noted:

> Then I witnessed what Brehm has described, for monkey after monkey, with head raised high and turned on one side, could not resist taking momentary peeps into the upright bag, at the dreadful object lying quiet at the bottom.[‡]

[†] Alfred Brehm, *Brehm's Life of Animals*, trans. from the 3rd German ed. as edited by Prof. Dr Pechuël-Loesche & Dr William Haacke, and rev. & abr. by Prof. Richard Schmidtlein (A. N. Marquis, 1895), 32.
[‡] Charles Darwin, *The Descent of Man: And Selection in Relation to Sex* (John Murray, 1871), vol. I, 42.
» Related to this may be the urge to read the private letters, diaries, or emails of someone close to you, despite the possibility that so doing could cause you pain.

Vertrautheitsbehagen

fair-trout-hites – beh-ha-ghen

~

Articles and affections worn comfortably smooth by time.

INTIMACY-CONTENTMENT

Irreaffentittenturbosuperdupertyp

ihr-reh-ahf-fen – tit-ten – toor-boh – zoo-per-doo-per – toop

~

Simpatico.

MAD-MONKEY-TITS-TURBO-SUPER-DUPER-GUY

Bammelbegierde

bahm-mel – beh-gear-duh

~

Inexorable attraction to something you fear or find unpleasant.

FEAR-DESIRE

31 For Lin Yutang, such envy has existential qualities:

> The world is therefore pretty much like an *à la carte* restaurant where everybody thinks the food the next table has ordered is so much more inviting and delicious than his own.[†]

† Lin Yutang, *The Importance of Living* (John Day, 1937), 74.

» Bizarrely, even guards at Guantánamo Bay experienced a form of *Mahlneid*: "Food envy was also alive and well. Troops stationed at the base in 2006 complained to me that the detainees were fed fresh strawberries while U.S. personnel had to settle for canned fruits." Karen J. Greenberg, *The Least Worst Place: Guantanamo's First 100 Days* (Oxford University Press, 2009), 110.

☙ *Futterneid* ("fodder envy") is also used in this context, although this term has zoological associations relating to how animals compete for, hoard, and hide food. See, for example, Stephen B. Vander Wall, *Food Hoarding in Animals* (University of Chicago Press, 1990). Erwin Bayer demonstrated that a chicken that had just gorged itself to satiety on grain would urgently start eating again if it saw another chicken begin to eat. Erwin Bayer, "Beiträge zur Zweikomponententheorie des Hungers," *Zeitschrift für Psychologie* 112 (1929): 1–54.

32 However, as Christopher Gasson pointed out, "it is almost impossible to determine whether readers are loyal to a paper because they enjoy reading it or because they simply like it better than the other options."[†]

Oscar Wilde touched on this in *An Ideal Husband*:

LORD CAVERSHAM: I suppose you have read *The Times* this morning?

LORD GORING (*airily*): *The Times*? Certainly not. I only read *The Morning Post*. All that one should know about modern life is where the Duchesses are; anything else is quite demoralizing.[‡]

† Christopher Gasson, *Media Equities: Evaluation and Trading* (Woodhead, 1996), 72.

‡ Oscar Wilde, *An Ideal Husband*, 1895, A IV.

» Thomas Jefferson took an absolutist position, as he explained in a letter dated 1 v 1794: "I do not take a single newspaper, nor read one a month; and I feel myself infinitely the happier for it." *The Writings of Thomas Jefferson*, vol. 4 (John C. Riker, 1854), 105.

33 There comes a time, in every man's haircut, when a mirror is flourished behind his head, and the inevitable (rhetorical) question is posed: "Will that do, sir?"

> How on earth do I know if it will do, with my hair unbrushed and in disorder? It is his business, not mine. He is a hair-cutter and ought surely to know when to stop. I give an evasive answer, and say, "I suppose so."

This is an extract from a long and vigorously splenetic essay on visiting the barber, from 1847. Its anonymous author introduces the subject by warning, "I tell you fairly that I consider hair-cutting one of the severest of the most periodical tortures to which unhappy man is subjected."[†]

† Anon., in *The London Sketch-Book*, June 1847, 16–19.

☙ *Haarmonie* plays on *Haar* ("hair") and *Harmonie* ("harmony") – a fact appreciated by a number of German hairdressers.

31
☞ 101

Mahlneid

mahl-nide

⌄

Coveting thy neighbour's restaurant order.

MEAL-ENVY

32

Zeitungsdünkel

tsy-toongs – duun-kel

⌄

Consternation that people read a newspaper you disapprove of.

NEWSPAPER-ARROGANCE

33

Haarmonie

hahr-moh-nee

⌄

Reassuring your hairdresser.

HA(I)RMONY

34 Even Barack Obama is not immune from wanting everyone to appreciate a gag he is proud of. When, on December 13, 2010, he signed the Healthy, Hunger-Free Kids Act into law, the President joked at his wife Michelle's expense, "Had I not been able to get this passed I'd be sleeping on the couch." The *New York Times* correspondent Jodi Kantor witnessed the event:

> He was momentarily lifting the curtain of her polished public image, hinting at the force of her disapproval, as if he wanted to let others know what he faced at home. He repeated the joke, to make sure everyone had heard. "We won't go into that," the first lady said, looking embarrassed.[†]

---

† Jodi Kantor, *The Obamas* (Hachette Digital, 2012), eBook.
» While simply repeating jokes is frowned upon by comedians, "reincorporation" is a central element of improvisation. "If you use something or mention something in the beginning of a scene, use it or mention it again somewhere else. Audiences find this deeply, deeply satisfying." Dan Diggles, *Improv for Actors* (Allworth Press, 2004), 90.

35 In *Sir Gawain and the Green Knight*, Sir Gawain feigns sleep in an effort to avoid the Lady of the castle:

> Hit watȝ þe ladi, loflyest to be-holde,
> It was the lady, the loveliest to behold,
> Þat droȝ þe dor after hir ful dernley & stylle,   [1188]
> That drew the door after her secretly and silently
> & boȝed to-warde þe bed; & þe burne schamed,
> And bowed toward the bed; and the knight [armour] ashamed
> & layde hym doun lystyly, & let as he slepte.
> And laid himself down lightly, and feigned sleep.
> & ho stepped stilly, & stel to his bedde,
> And she stepped silently, and stole to his bed,
> Keste vp þe cortyn, & creped with-inne,   [1192]
> Lifted up the curtain, and crept within,
> & set hir ful softly on þe bed-syde,
> And sat herself softly on the bedside.
> & lenged þere selly longe, to loke quen he wakened.[†]
> And waited there strangely [?] long, to see when he awoke.

---

† *Sir Gawain and the Green Knight* (*c*.1370–1400?), ed. Richard Morris (Kegan Paul, Trench, Trübner, 1864), 38.
➤ See Jacob & Wilhelm Grimm, "Dornröschen" (KHM 50).

36 Although the term "rubbernecking" is now used almost exclusively to describe gawping at road traffic accidents, its original use was associated with tourism and sightseeing in America. *The Oxford English Dictionary* dates the word's origin to 1894 America, and H. L. Mencken observed: "Such a term as *rubber-neck* is almost a complete treatise on American psychology; it reveals the national habit of mind more clearly than any labored inquiry could ever reveal it."[†]

Curiously, in 1928, D. H. Lawrence used "rubberneck" in a sense similar to "brassneck": "There was a toughness, a curious rubber-necked toughness and unlivingness about the middle and upper classes."[‡]

---

† H. L. Mencken, *The American Language* (Knopf, 1921), 31.
‡ D. H. Lawrence, *Lady Chatterley's Lover* (1928) (Penguin, 1994), 141.
➤ The jocular German term for a hairpin bend is *Schwiegermutterkurve* ("mother-in-law curve"), which presumably derives from the potential for disposing of an unloved relative by judiciously opening the car door while navigating a sharp corner.

Witzbeharrsamkeit

vits – beh-hahr-zahm-kite

~

Unashamedly repeating a *bon mot* until it is properly heard by everyone present.

JOKE-INSISTENCE

Dornhöschenschlaf

dorn – hoos-sh'yen – shlahf

~

Feigning sleep to avoid unwanted sexual intimacy.

THORNY-LINGERIE-SLEEP

Schwiegermutterkurvenlanghals

shvee-gher-moot-ter – kuhr-fen – lahng-hahls

~

The morbid urge to slow down and ſtare at a road accident.

MOTHER-IN-LAW-BEND-LONG-NECK

37 This portmanteau-portmanteau relates to a host of numerical (and numerological) curiosities, such as:

Painstakingly watching the pump's gauge when filling up with petrol, so the total halts at a round number.[†] The significance of remembering a paramour's phone number (rendered pretty much obsolete by new technology). ❦ Setting an alarm to an odd/even/lucky time.[‡] (☞ 118) ❦ Misdating documents well into the new year.[*] ❦ When an odometer rolls onto a pleasing number. ❦ Incorporating birthdays into passwords or PINs. ❦ Satisfaction in palindromic or otherwise elegant dates and times. ❦ Ending a taxi journey prematurely to avoid breaking a large banknote (or because you're running out of cash). ❦ Mental tricks to remember numbers. ❦ The bizarre lure of numerical coincidence for conspiracy theorists.[§]

[†] "Often I'm disappointed: the number will stop at $16.01 or even $16.02 – seldom below. But no, yesterday the numbers stopped dead on $16.00, and I said, 'Bingo, baby.'" Nicholson Baker, *A Box of Matches* (Vintage, 2003), 147.
[‡] "There is divinity in odd numbers." William Shakespeare, *The Merry Wives of Windsor*, 1602, A v, S i.

[*] "How strange at first it seems to us, instead of 1858 to write 1859. ... This fact has often awakened in our minds a warm sympathy with those ladies who at a certain period of their lives are necessitated one day to write their names the old way and the next the new way!" H. Harbaugh, "The New Year," *The Guardian: A Monthly Magazine*, vol. 10 (Pearsol & Geist, 1859), 29.
[§] "With numbers you can do anything you like." Umberto Eco, *Foucault's Pendulum* (1988), trans. W. Weaver (Harvest, 2007), 279.
↝ *Schnapszahl* ("schnapps number") is a number with repeating digits, akin to the double vision precipitated by excess schnapps.

· · ·

38 J. H. McDermott noted two key characteristics of "annoying sounds," in addition to volume:

SHARPNESS (energy at high frequencies, e.g., 2–4 kHz)
ROUGHNESS (fluctuations between ~20–200 Hz)[†]

[†] J. H. McDermott, "Auditory Preferences and Aesthetics," in *Neuroscience of Preference and Choice*, eds. R. J. Dolan & T. Sharot (Academic Press, 2012), 228–29.

39 A range of technical terms are used in this field:[†]

BAULKING · Refusing even to join a long or slow queue.

JOCKEYING · Strategically moving between queues.

RENEGING · Quitting a queue before reaching the end.

COLLUSION · When one queuer represents others, who congregate at the point of resolution; or when several members of a party join different queues to achieve the fastest resolution; or when a queuer sells his place (either because he is spontaneously offered money, or because he is a "professional queuer"[†]).

[†] See, for example, Joti Lal Jain, Sri Gopal Mohanty, & Walter Böhm, *A Course on Queuing Models* (CRC Press, 2007), 57.
[‡] In 1922, London theatre ticket queuers charged 1'6 an hour.[*] More recently, professional queuers (跑腿) in China charge *c*.$3 an hour – reflecting the country's wealth inequality and its "lazy economy" (懒惰经济).[§]
[*] "Professional 'Queuers,'" *The Pittsburgh Press*, 13 iv 1922, 6;
[§] *All Things Considered*, NPR, 25 vii 2011, n.pr/ogwszN.

Schnapszahlbesessenheit

shnahps-tsahl – beh-zess-en-hite

~

A preoccupation with certain numbers or numerical phenomena.

SCHNAPPS-NUMBER-OBSESSION

Fingernageltafelquietschen

fing-er-nah-ghel – tah-fel – kveetch-en

~

The visceral hatred of certain noises.

FINGERNAIL-BLACKBOARD-SQUEAL

Aktivansteher

ahk-teev – ahn-shteh-er

~

One skilled in the various techniques of queuing.

ENERGETIC-QUEUER

40 We can turn to the adolescence of Louis XIV – the Sun King of France – to see what happens when accidental spitting is *not* ignored:

> A curious scene … took place in consequence of Louis being obliged to sleep in the same room with his brother, the Duke of Anjou. On waking in the morning, the king accidentally spat upon the bed of his brother, who, a quick and passionate boy, immediately spat upon that of Louis in return: the king replied by spitting in his brother's face; from which they proceeded to still more nasty marks of their indignation against each other. Having, at length, exhausted their powers in that way, they tore the clothes off each other's beds, and ended by a pitched battle.[†]

---

† G. P. R. James, *The Life and Times of Louis the Fourteenth* (George Bell, 1874), vol. 1, 394.

» On 28 i 1661, Samuel Pepys was accidentally spat on, "but after seeing her to be a very pretty lady, I was not troubled at it at all." *The Diary of Samuel Pepys* (Dodd, Mead, 1884), vol. 1, 325.

41 Charles Dickens captured this sensation perfectly:

> When I had got all my responsibilities down upon my list, I compared each with the bill, and ticked it off. My self-approval when I ticked an entry was quite a luxurious sensation.[†]

---

† Charles Dickens, *Great Expectations* (Riverside Press, 1874), 49.

» A notoriously fatal list appears in Gilbert and Sullivan's *The Mikado* (1885). In Act 1, Ko-Ko (Lord High Executioner of Titipu) sings a song that contains a "little list" of "society offenders" who "never would be missed" if executed – including "people who have flabby hands" and "the lady novelist." A tradition has developed of updating this list – both to expurgate the N-word, which is in the original, and to add topical gags. A 1921 performance at the Prince's Theatre, London, included on the list "the prohibitionist";[‡] a 1933 performance at the Theatre Royal, Sydney, Australia, included "the leg-theorist," a reference to the "bodyline" cricket controversy;[*] and a 1941 performance at His Majesty's Theatre, Melbourne, Australia, included the "petrol-rationist," "sly fifth-columnist," and "pseudo-pacifist."[§]

‡ *The Times*, 20 xii 1921, 8; * *The Sydney Mail*, 1 ii 1933, 28;

§ *The Age*, 1 ix 1941, 6.

42 Although William M. Thackeray claimed that the agony of laughter was "impossible to describe in words,"[†] the c16th French physician Laurent Joubert came close, in his canonical *Treatise on Laughter*:

> Everyone can clearly see, with laughter, suddenly the face moves, the mouth enlarges, the eyes sparkle and water, the cheeks blush, the chest shakes, we cannot speak, and when this goes on for a while, the veins of the neck bulge, the arms wave, and the legs stamp, the gut spasms painfully: we cough, perspire, piss and shit ourselves through laughter, and sometimes we even pass out.[‡]

---

† W. M. Thackeray, *Men's Wives* (D. Appleton, 1852), 137.

‡ Laurent Joubert, *Traité du Ris* (Nicolas Chesneau, 1579), 42.

» "Not through wrath does one slayeth, but by laughter." Friedrich Nietzsche, *Also sprach Zarathustra* (C. G. Naumann, 1895), 458.

➻ It is disputed whether Zeuxis (fl. c5th B.C.) did actually die laughing, after he painted a particularly ugly woman. See, for example, Carlo Dati, *Vite de Pittori Antichi* (Florence, 1667), 40.

Speichelgleichmut

shpy-cchel – glycch-moot

~

Pretending you haven't been accidentally spat on in conversation.

SALIVA-STOICISM

Entlistungsfreude

ent-liss-toongs – froy-duh

~

The sense of satisfaction afforded by crossing things off lists.

DE-LISTING-JOY

Zeuxisgelächter

tsoy-xiss – gheh-lecch-ter

~

Laughter so prolonged and intense it causes physical pain.

ZEUXIS-LAUGHTER

43 This portmanteau-portmanteau describes a range of phenomena specifically related to alcohol(ism):

❧ The point of perfect tipsiness. ❧ Downing a shot you don't want. ❧ Sobriety in the company of inebriates.[†] ❧ Swearing you will never drink again. ❧ A heartfelt toast. ❧ Falling off / clambering on the wagon. ❧ Fake-drinking.[‡] ❧ Drunkenly telling others you're not drunk. ❧ Drunkenly telling yourself you're not drunk. ❧ Pleasurable bits of bar "business" (toothpick tricks, napkin sculpture, &c.).[*] (☏8) ❧ Coaxing a smile out of a curmudgeonly barman.[§] ❧ Beer goggles. ❧ Getting a drink on the house.[‡] ❧ Fine drinks in absurd glasses. ❧ An after-hours "lock-in." ❧ Successfully improvising a corkscrew or bottle opener. ❧ When gesticulation is the thief of wine. ❧ An Irish pub singalong.[∴] ❧ The complexities of bringing very cheap or very expensive wine to a party. ❧ Buying a drink for the barman.[⁝] ❧ In vino veritas.[®] ❧ In vino improbitas. ❧ An experience with a spirit that renders it thereafter undrinkable.

---

† And vice versa. Oliver Reed said, "I do not live in the world of sobriety." Robert Sellers, *Hellraisers* (Thomas Dunne, 2009), 136.

‡ Nelson Mandela "fake-drank" when given a tumbler of whisky by F. W. de Klerk to celebrate his imminent release from prison: "I raised the glass in a toast, but only pretended to drink; such spirits are too strong for me." Nelson Mandela, *Long Walk to Freedom* (Hachette Digital, 2008), eBook.

* See, for example, Paul Zenon, *Bar Tricks* (Five Mile Press, 2008).

§ A man's desire to "ingratiate himself with the barman" is one "which barmen inspire as readily as traffic policemen, first officers of ocean liners, and the examining doctors of life-insurance companies." Eric Linklater, *A Man Over Forty* (Macmillan, 1963), 104.

‡ Rosie Schaap wrote in her thirst-inducing memoir, "Never *ask* for a freebie. That's up to the bartender – not you. (As one Brooklyn barman I know memorably put it, 'Buybacks are like blow jobs. If you have to ask for one, you don't deserve one.')" *Drinking with Men* (Riverhead Books, 2013), 103.

∴ Of course, there's Irish and "Oirish." Sean Williams noted, "Singing a song in Irish frequently leads to the request for a 'real Irish' song (in other words, an Irish-themed American song)." *Focus: Traditional Irish Music* (Routledge, 2010), 6.

⁝ Kate Fox explored how to buy the barman a drink in a British pub in *Watching the English* (Hodder & Stoughton, 2004).

® Samuel Johnson argued that this motto was "useless to a man who knew he was not a liar when he was sober." See *Johnsoniana*, ed. Robina Napier (George Bell, 1884), 97–98.

44 In Fyodor Dostoevsky's *The Brothers Karamazov*, Nikolay Ivanovitch Krassotkin complains, "Of course I hate my name Nikolay. … It's so trivial, so ordinary."[†] Perhaps literature's most celebrated discussion of disliking one's name appears in *Romeo and Juliet*:

JULIET: O Romeo, Romeo! wherefore art thou
    Romeo?
    Deny thy father, and refuse thy name;
    Or, if thou wilt not, be but sworn my love,
    And I'll no longer be a Capulet.
    […]
ROMEO: … My name, dear saint, is hateful to myself,
    Because it is an enemy to thee;
    Had I written it, I would tear the word.[‡]

---

† Fyodor Dostoevsky, *The Brothers Karamazov* (1880), trans. Constance Garnett (Macmillan, 1922), 577.

‡ William Shakespeare, *Romeo and Juliet*, 1597, A II, S ii.

» The rapper Eminem told *Rolling Stone* in 2002 that he "fucking hate[s]" his career-launching 1999 single, "My Name Is." See Anthony Bozza, *Whatever You Say I Am: The Life and Times of Eminem* (2003) (Three Rivers Press, 2010), eBook.

43

Spirituosenhandlung

shpih-rih-too-oh-zen – hahnd-loong

The incidents and accidents caused by alcohol.

LIQUOR-ACTION

44

Eigennamenhass

eye-ghen-nah-men – hahss

Being embarrassed by, bored with, or otherwise disliking your name.

PROPER-NAME-HATRED

45
{✗}
☞ 106

Plauschplage

plowsh – plah-ghe

The pressure to make bantering small talk with people you interact with every day.

PRATTLE-PLAGUE

46 This tendency is illustrated by one of literature's vainest motorists, Mr Toad, of Toad Hall:

> The motor-car went Poop-poop-poop,
>   As it raced along the road.
> Who was it steered it into a pond?
>   Ingenious Mr Toad![†]

One of literature's vainest cars appears in *The Great Gatsby*, in which, as Malcolm Cowley noted, "the characters are visibly represented by the cars they drive."[‡] It is no accident that Gatsby's "circus-wagon" ("death car") is "a rich cream color, bright with nickel, swollen here and there in its monstrous length with triumphant hat boxes and supper-boxes and tool-boxes …"[*]

[†] Kenneth Grahame, *The Wind in the Willows* (Charles Scribner's Sons, 1908), 244.
[‡] Malcom Cowley, "The Romance of Money," in *F. Scott Fitzgerald*, ed. Harold Bloom (Chelsea House, 2001), 99.
[*] F. Scott Fitzgerald, *The Great Gatsby* (1925) (Penguin, 2000), 63.
↝ "Pagoda" refers to the concave roof of the Mercedes 230SL, and some of its successors, which vaguely resembles a Chinese pagoda.

47 The power of photographs to evoke memories was commented on both by Ray Davies[†] and, earlier, by Sigmund Freud:

> In the photographic camera [man] has created an instrument which retains the fleeting visual impressions, just as a gramophone disc retains the equally fleeting auditory ones; both are at bottom materializations of the power he possesses of recollection, his memory.[‡]

[†] Ray Davies, "Picture Book," *The Kinks Are the Village Green Preservation Society* (Pye Records, 1968).
[‡] Sigmund Freud, *Civilization and Its Discontents* (1930), trans. & ed. James Strachey (W. W. Norton, 1989), 43.
↝ The camera manufacturer Rollei began life in 1920, when Paul Franke and Reinhold Heidecke founded the Werkstatt für Feinmechanik und Optik, in Braunschweig, Germany. Although *Rückblende* translates as "flashback," the element *Blende* also refers to an optical diaphragm.

48 Many have argued that we should take pleasure in all seasons, rather than yearning for light and warmth and loathing darkness and cold – not least Samuel Johnson: "to call upon the sun for peace and gaiety, or deprecate the clouds lest sorrow should overwhelm us, is the cowardice of idleness, and the idolatry of folly."[†]

William Shakespeare expressed a similar sentiment:

> At Christmas I no more desire a rose
> Than wish a snow in May's newfangled shows;
> But like of each thing that in season grows.[‡]

As did George Santayana: "To be interested in the changing seasons is … a happier state of mind than to be hopelessly in love with spring."[*]

[†] Samuel Johnson, *The Idler* № 11 (24 vi 1758).
[‡] William Shakespeare, *Love's Labour's Lost*, 1598, A I, S i.
[*] George Santayana, *The Life of Reason or The Phases of Human Progress: Reason in Art* (Charles Scribner's Sons, 1905), 189.
↝ See Richard Wagner, *Die Walküre* (wwv 86B) (c.1856), especially "Winterstürme wichen dem Wonnemond," in A I, S iii.

46 Pagodeneitelkeit

pah-go-den – eye-tel-kite

The smug self-satisfaction of those behind the wheel of a vintage car.

PAGODA-VANITY

47 Rolleirückblende

rohl-eye – ruuk-blen-duh

The flood of memory released when looking at old photos.

ROLLEI-FLASHBACK

48 Wintersturmwonnemondwende

vin-ter-shtoorm – vohn-neh-mohndt – ven-duh

Delight at the changing of the seasons.

WINTER-STORM-BLISS-MOON-TURNING

Schattenfreude

49 In a powerful essay dissecting the macabre appetite for images of Detroit's economic collapse, John Patrick Leary listed some of the tropes of "ruin porn":

> The exuberant connoisseurship of dereliction; the unembarrassed rejoicing at the "excitement" of it all, hastily balanced by the liberal posturing of sympathy for a "man-made Katrina"; and most importantly, the absence of people other than … "street zombies."[†]

Our perverse pleasure in sumptuous images of squalor was also denounced by the legendary impresario of Rio de Janeiro's Carnival, Joãosinho Trinta:

> The people like luxury; it's the intellectuals who like misery.[‡]

[†] John Patrick Leary, "Detroitism," *Guernica*, 15 i 2011, bit.ly/I0IphI.
[‡] *"O povo gosta de luxo; quem gosta de miséria é intelectual."* Quoted in Paulo Buchsbaum, *Frases Geniais* [Genius Phrases] (Ediouro Publicações, 2004), 396.

50 The humorist Robert Benchley skewered this terrible ennui: "Sunday morning may be cheery enough, with its extra cup of coffee and litter of Sunday newspapers, but there is always hanging over it the ominous threat of 3 p.m., when the sun gets around to the back windows and Life stops dead in its tracks."[†]

[†] Robert Benchley, *The Treasurer's Report: And Other Aspects of Community Singing* (Harper & Brothers, 1930), 90.
» In 1919, the Hungarian psychoanalyst Sándor Ferenczi devised the diagnosis "Sunday neuroses" (*vasárnapi neurózisok*) to explain why patients had headaches and stomach pains unrelated to Sundays' "longer sleep and better meals." Citing his friend Sigmund Freud, Ferenczi argued that for most people, Sundays offered *external* freedom from "duties and compulsions" and *internal* freedom from "permanently repressed instincts." But this was not so for the "neurotically disposed," whose "repressed impulses" and "self-punishment fantasies" were "mobilized against them" on the Sabbath, manifesting in "little hysterical symptoms." See Sándor Ferenczi, *Further Contributions to the Theory and Technique of Psycho-Analysis* (Hogarth Press, 1950), 174–77.
➷ *Sonntagsleerung* is the term used by the German postal service to denote a Sunday collection of mail.

51 There is a wealth of research into our ability to re-enter dreams once woken, and the phenomenon of incorporating environmental stimuli (e.g., an alarm) into dreams. Indeed, as Antrobus et al. wrote:

> The question – awake or asleep – is not a particularly useful one. Even though we have two discrete words – sleep and wakefulness – this does not mean that the behaviour associated with the words can be forced into two discrete categories. … At a given moment, all systems of the organism are not necessarily equally asleep or awake.[†]

[†] Judith S. Antrobus, John S. Antrobus, & Charles Fisher, "Discrimination of Dreaming and Nondreaming Sleep," *Archives of General Psychiatry* 12, № 4 (1965): 395–401.
» If we are to believe the poet's account, in 1797 Samuel Taylor Coleridge conceived "Kubla Khan" while in a drug-induced stupor. On waking, he set about writing the lines he had dreamt, before he was interrupted by a "person on business from Porlock," who disastrously derailed his train of thought (☞ 116) and shattered all but a few "scattered lines and images" of his vision.

49 Ruinenpornographie

roo-een-en – por-no-grah-fee

A morbid fascination with photographs of contemporary urban decay.

RUIN-PORNOGRAPHY

50 Sonntagsleerung

zohn-tahgs – leh-roong

Sunday-afternoon depression.

SUNDAY-EMPTYING

51 Traumneustartversuch

traowm – noy-shtahrt – fair-zoocch

The (usually futile) attempt to return to the plot of a dream after having been woken.

DREAM-RESTART-EXPERIMENT

52 Fake surprise tends to be faked for far too long, according to the acclaimed psychologist Paul Ekman:

> Surprise is always a very brief emotion, lasting only until the surprised person has figured out the unexpected event. While most people know how to fake surprise, few could do so convincingly with the fast onset and offset that a natural surprise must have.[†]

Charles Darwin noted that "a person may often be seen to pretend surprise by merely raising his eyebrows," and listed these five stages of genuine surprise:

> *Attention*, if sudden and close, graduates into *surprise*; and this into *astonishment*; and this into stupefied *amazement*. The latter frame of mind is closely akin to *terror*.[‡]

[†] Paul Ekman, *Telling Lies: Clues to Deceit in the Marketplace, Politics, and Marriage* (1991) (W. W. Norton, 2009), 148.
[‡] Charles Darwin, *The Expression of the Emotions in Man and Animals* (1872) (D. Appleton, 1886), 278; italics added.

53 In the Jewish faith, this "storm before the calm" is known as *'aninut*. During *'aninut*, the seven *'onenim*[†] most directly bereaved are excused from certain religious duties (saying some prayers, wearing ceremonial garments, &c.) and prohibited from certain actions (eating meat, drinking alcohol, doing business, &c.). The respite that *'aninut* provides allows those closest to the deceased to plan the funeral and to show appropriate respect for the dead without distraction.

[†] The father, mother, son, daughter, brother, sister, and spouse of the deceased. See Isaac Klein, *A Guide to Jewish Religious Practice* (1979) (Jewish Theological Seminary of America, 1992), 274.
» "[Mourning] is a transitional period for the survivors, and they enter it through rites of separation and emerge from it through rites of reintegration into society (rites of the lifting of mourning). In some cases, the transitional period of the living is a counterpart of the transitional period of the deceased, and the termination of the first sometimes coincides with the termination of the second – that is, with the incorporation of the deceased into the world of the dead." Arnold van Gennep, *The Rites of Passage* (1908), trans. Monika B. Vizedom & Gabrielle L. Caffee (University of Chicago Press, 1960), 147.

54 For Louis Savot, symmetry was uniquely human:

> Animals know how to choose as well as men, and sometimes better, the convenience of their homes and haunts. But they cannot create the grace of symmetry, since knowledge of order and proportion belongs, of all the animals, to man alone – who also receives alone the satisfaction and joy of these things.[†]

For Montesquieu, symmetry was a functional pleasure:

> Where *Symmetry* is … useful to the mind, by aiding its comprehension, and facilitating its operations and its perceptions, there it is, and must always be agreeable; but where it does not produce this effect, it becomes flat and insipid, because, without any good purpose, it deprives an object of that *variety* to which nature has given superior charms.[‡]

[†] Louis Savot, *L'Architecture Françoise … [sic]* (Paris, 1624), 205.
[‡] In Alexander Gerard, *An Essay on Taste* (Edinburgh, 1764), 268.

Überraschungspartyüberraschungsheuchelei

uu-ber-rah-shoongs-pahr-tee – uu-ber-rah-shoongs-hoy-cchel-eye

Feigning surprise at a surprise party.

SURPRISE-PARTY-SURPRISE-HYPOCRISY

Vorruhesturm

for-roo-eh-shtoorm

The fugue state between a death and the funeral.

PRE-CALM-STORM

Ebenmäßigkeitsentzückung

eh-ben-mess-ig-kites – ent-tsuu-koong

The profound sense of satisfaction afforded by symmetry.

WELL-PROPORTION-DELIGHT

Schattenfreude

55 The psychiatrist Charles Sidney Bluemel associated this impulse with Adam and Eve's temptation to eat the forbidden fruit in the Garden of Eden.[†]

In *The Winter's Tale*, Leontes is restrained from kissing (what may or may not be) a statue of his wife, Hermione, by the threat of wet paint:

LEONTES: … What fine chisel
 Could ever yet cut breath? Let no man mock me,
 For I will kiss her.

PAULINA: Good my lord, forbear:
 The ruddiness upon her lip is wet.
 You'll mar it if you kiss it, stain your own
 With oily painting.[‡]

[†] C. S. Bluemel, *Psychiatry and Common Sense* (Macmillan, 1954), 215. Splendidly, he added: "The painter is in trouble in this situation, and he writes such signs as 'Wet paint; believe the painter.'"
[‡] William Shakespeare, *The Winter's Tale*, c.1610, A v, S iii.
➻ The *vernissage* ("varnishing") was traditionally a day to varnish and retouch paintings prior to the opening of a show.

56 The bizarre satisfaction some (often very literate) people take in being unable to perform basic arithmetic was nailed by the mathematician John Allen Paulos:

> The same people who cringe when words such as "imply" and "infer" are confused react without a trace of embarrassment to even the most egregious of numerical solecisms.… Part of the reason for this perverse pride in mathematical ignorance is that its consequences are not usually as obvious as are those of other weaknesses.[†]

[†] John Allen Paulos, *Innumeracy: Mathematical Illiteracy and Its Consequences* (Hill & Wang, 2001), 4. And John Mighton wryly observed: "Many people are convinced that there is a gene for mathematics. This gene seems to come with an expiry date, though, and most people can remember the year it gave out." *The End of Ignorance* (Vintage Canada, 2008), 25.
➻ *Einmaleins* ("one times one") is the German "multiplication table." *Das kleine Einmaleins* is the table of all products of integers up to 10; *das große Einmaleins* is this table, up to 20. German primary school pupils learn *das kleine Einmaleins* by heart; thus *Einmaleins* is used figuratively to describe "the basics."

57 This pulse of contentment comes from finding a solution we *know* to be correct, since the puzzle's rubric supplies its own confirmation. Furthermore, as V. S. Ramachandran explained, such pulses are a fleeting form of bliss: "Whenever we successfully solve a puzzle, we get rewarded with a zap of pleasure."[†]

Some of the most popular graphic design offers the same kind of "zap," by presenting a visual enigma for the consumer to decode. A rightly celebrated example is the forward arrow formed by the "negative space" between the "E" and the "x" of the FedEx logo. Less known is an equally clever design for the Guild of Food Writers, shown here.[‡]

[†] V. S. Ramachandran, *The Tell-Tale Brain: A Neuroscientist's Quest for What Makes Us Human* (W. W. Norton, 2012), 228.
[‡] Designed by 300 Million. Reproduced with permission.
» See, for example, Beryl McAlhone and David Stuart's superb (and superbly titled) *A Smile in the Mind* (Phaidon, 1996).
➻ A contraction of *Irrgarten* ("maze") and *Erleuchtung* ("enlightenment").

Vernissageversuchung

vehr-niss-sarje – fair-zoo-cchoong

~

The urge to test whether paint marked "wet paint" really is still wet.

VERNISSAGE-TEMPTATION

Einmaleinswiedergabeschwächenstolz

ine-mahl-ines – vee-der-gah-beh – shveh-cchen-shtolts

~

Pride at your innumeracy.

MULTIPLICATION-TABLE-REPRODUCTION-IMPAIRMENT-PRIDE

Irrleuchtung

ihr-loycch-toong

~

The surge of pleasure experienced as you solve, say, a crossword clue.

MAZE-MENT

58 Our ability to "tune in" to a single audio stream within a cacophony is known to acousticians as the "cocktail party effect," since that is where acousticians like to hang out. Research by Aubin et al. indicates that this effect also plays a vital role in the life of *Aptenodytes patagonicus* (the king penguin), which breeds, without nests, surrounded by many thousand fellow penguins:

> The ability of the chick to perform parent identification in such a constraining environment results not only in its capacity to reduce the distance of communication within a rendezvous site, but also in its exceptional sensorial capacity to discriminate in spite of the masking effect of the colonial life.[†]

† Thierry Aubin & Pierre Jouventin, "Cocktail-Party Effect in King Penguin Colonies," *Proceedings of the Royal Society B* 265, № 1406 (Sep 1998): 1665–73.
↝ *Lauschangriff* combines the subtlety of "eavesdropping" with the violence of "attack." In the 1990s, Germany's security services launched a controversial acoustic surveillance programme of private residences, known as Großer ("great") Lauschangriff.

59 This nagging sense of loose-endedness – termed "indigestion in the mind" by the Tibetan Buddhist Chögyam Trungpa[†] – was noted by Tom Stoppard:

> The encounter felt incomplete, in the way that his brain signalled incompletion when he left [a] half-eaten sandwich lying around.[‡]

† Chögyam Trungpa, *Smile at Fear: Awakening the True Heart of Bravery*, ed. Carolyn Rose Gimian (Shambhala, 2009), 47.
‡ Tom Stoppard, *Lord Malquist and Mr Moon* (1966) (Faber & Faber, 1992), 36.
↝ *Zeigarnikfrustration* derives from the work of the Russian psychiatrist Bluma Wulfovna Zeigarnik, who established that people remembered interrupted tasks better than tasks they had completed. Although this became known as the "Zeigarnik Effect" (Эффект Зейгарник), the idea was prompted by Zeigarnik's German supervisor, Kurt Lewin, who was intrigued by restaurant waiters who could remember complex orders for the duration of the meal (without taking notes), but would forget them as soon as they had calculated the bill. See Bluma Zeigarnik, "Über das Behalten von erledigten und unerledigten Handlungen," *Psychologische Forschung* 9 (1927): 1–85.

60 In 2009, the Nobel Prize-winning economist Paul Krugman outlined the characteristics of "Serious Person Syndrome, aka it's better to have been conventionally wrong than unconventionally right":

> Thus, you're not considered serious on national security unless you bought the case for invading Iraq, even though the skeptics were completely right; you're not considered a serious political commentator unless you dismissed all the things those reflexive anti-Bushists were saying, even though they all turn out to have been true; and you're not considered serious about economic policy unless you dismissed warnings about a housing bubble and waved off worries about future crises.[†]

† Paul Krugman, "On the Reappointment of Ben Bernanke," (blog), *The New York Times*, 25 viii 2009, nyti.ms/rGdbW.
↝ Hanswurst ("John Sausage") is a stock-character buffoon – dating to *c.*1519 – similar to Jean Potage, Pickelhäring, Signor Macaroni, Paprika Jancsi, and Jack Pudding.

58
☞ 106

Fetenlauschangriff

feh-ten – laowssh-ahn-griff

~

Tuning in and out of a number of conversations at a party.

PARTY-EAVESDROPPING-ATTACK

59
☞ 116

Zeigarnikfrustration

tsay-gar-nick – froo-strah-tsyohn

~

The gnawing sense of incompleteness knowing there is a partially eaten snack lying around somewhere.

ZEIGARNIK-FRUSTRATION

60

Hanswursthochschätzung

hahnz-voorst – hohcch-sheht-tsoong

~

The respect conferred on those who are conventionally wrong rather than unconventionally right.

DUNDERHEAD-ESTEEM

Schattenfreude

62 Every city has a handful of jinxed locations, which, like Sirens luring sailors, draw one restaurateur after another onto the rocks. In December 2010, New York Burger Co. opened a new Manhattan location on the corner of 23rd and 10th. This site had seen at least four restaurants in a dozen years, including Le Solex, the owner of which, Robert Arbor, told *The New York Times*, "It is the Bermuda Triangle, the evil nest, my downfall, my only failure."[†] Taking no chances, New York Burger Co.'s operators hired a range of religious figures to bless their new venture. (Prompting, one assumes, the inevitable "A Catholic, a Jew, and a Buddhist walk into a burger joint" jokes.) At the time of writing, the restaurant appeared to be doing a roaring trade.

† Diane Cardwell, "A Blessing of the Burger to End a Restaurant Jinx," *The New York Times*, 6 xii 2010, nyti.ms/fyRcPj.
» Related is the (usually unfounded) conviction that suspiciously empty restaurants or shops "must be a front" for nefarious activity, rather than simply unpopular or badly run businesses.

63 One of the finest descriptions of pocket-patting comes in James Joyce's *Ulysses* – though here Leopold Bloom is (feigning) searching for a bar of lemon soap:

His hasty hand went quick into a pocket, took out, read unfolded Agendath Netaim. Where did I?
Busy looking for.
He thrust back quickly Agendath.
Afternoon she said.
I am looking for that. Yes, that. Try all pockets. Handker. *Freeman*. Where did I? Ah, yes. Trousers. Purse. Potato. Where did I?
Hurry. Walk quietly. Moment more. My heart.
His hand looking for the where did I put found in his hip pocket soap lotion have to call tepid paper stuck. Ah, soap there! Yes. Gate.
Safe![†]

† James Joyce, *Ulysses* (Shakespeare and Company, 1922), 175.
» Rudyard Kipling observed that "ticket-collecting is a slow business in the East, where people secrete their tickets in all sorts of curious places." *Kim* (1900–01) (Doubleday, Page, 1922), 46.

61

Beichtstuhldrang

byccht-shtool – drahng

~

The urge to confess.

CONFESSIONAL-IMPULSE

62

Gaststättenneueröffnungsuntergangsgewissheit

gahst-shteht-ten – noy-air-oeuf-noongs – oon-ter-gahngs – ghe-viss-hite

~

Total confidence that a newly opened restaurant is doomed to fail.

INN-NEW-OPENING-DOWNFALL-CERTITUDE

63

Dokumentverlustpanik

doh-koo-ment-fair-loost – pah-neek

~

Anxiously patting every pocket to locate a vital document you had just moments ago.

DOCUMENT-LOSS-PANIC

Schadenfreude

64 The consequences of this tendency were discussed by Gérald Sfez, in an essay on Machiavelli and evil:

> Cowardice in the face of evil, far from attenuating it, aggravates it, all the while diminishing good's power of repercussion, its intensity, even effacing all trace of this good by a sort of retroactive anaesthesia and amnesia.[†]

Many have damned the appeasement of Nazism as one of the C20th's most craven capitulations to evil. Yet A. J. P. Taylor, and others, perceived more nuance:

> Historians do a bad day's work when they write the appeasers off as stupid or as cowards. They were men confronted with real problems, doing their best in the circumstances of their time.[‡]

[†] Gérald Sfez, "Deciding on Evil," in *Radical Evil*, ed. Joan Copjec (Verso, 1996), 135.
[‡] A. J. P. Taylor, "Second Thoughts" (1963, preface), *The Origins of the Second World War* (1961) (Simon & Schuster, 2005), xxvi.

65 This sensation can make you question the entire scale of your remembered childhood – as the civil rights activist Elmer Gertz noted in his autobiography:

> "I want to see my old school," I said. I had not seen it in more than half a century. We drove past it. It was like a toy school, so much smaller than I remembered it, so much smaller than they now build schools. Were all of the giants of my past in fact pygmies?[†]

[†] Elmer Gertz, *To Life: The Story of a Chicago Lawyer* (1974) (McGraw-Hill, 1990), 13–14.
↝ *Dreikäsehoch* ("three cheeses high") is used to describe a small (and perhaps precocious) child no taller than three wheels of cheese stacked one atop another.

66 Although Geneen Roth does not actually recommend eating at the refrigerator in her book *When You Eat at the Refrigerator, Pull Up a Chair*, she does advocate pulling up a chair: "Sitting down allows you to concentrate and take pleasure from what you are doing. It also dispels the illusion that you are not really eating while you are standing."[†] ☙ In many families the fridge is a locus of communication. Debbie Nelson stuck lines of her poetry on the fridge when her son was at home.[‡] And carers of dementia patients are advised to label the fridge with pictures of milk.[*] Yet not all fridge messages are so positive. During the 1970 trial of Charles Manson and his followers for the Tate–LaBianca murders, it was disclosed that "healter [sic] skelter" was scrawled on a fridge door in one of the victims' blood.[§]

[†] Geneen Roth, *When You Eat at the Refrigerator, Pull Up a Chair* (Hyperion, 2010), eBook.
[‡] Debbie Nelson with Annette Witheridge, *My Son Marshall, My Son Eminem* (Phoenix Books, 2008), 74.
[*] Danny Walsh, *Dementia Care Training Manual* … (Jessica Kingsley, 2006), 73.
[§] *The New York Times*, 3 ix 1970, 15.

64

Bösewichtsduckmäusrigkeit

boo-ze-vicchts – dook-moyz-rihg-kite

˄

Cowardice in the face of malevolence.

VILLAIN-PUSILLANIMITY

65
27

Dreikäsehochregression

dry-keh-zuh-hocch – reh-greh-syohn

˄

Returning to your old school and finding everything feels so small.

SMALL-CHILD-REGRESSION

66
80

Kühlschrankblockade

kuul-shrahnk – bloh-kah-duh

˄

Staring at the refrigerator, hungry but unsure of what to eat.

FRIDGE-FREEZE

Schottenfreude

67 The writer and speaker Paul Hellman observed:

> I love being met at the airport, even by complete strangers. There they are, holding a sign with your name on it – it's as though they're out there campaigning for you to win an election.[†]

The curious corollary of this is the deflation experienced when no one greets you at the airport – unfairly felt when nobody knew you were arriving – which is a form of *Luftfahrtorigaminiedergeschlagenheit* (☜24).

[†] Paul Hellman, *Naked at Work (and Other Fears)* (New American Library, 2002), 106.
» Incidentally, in 2006, VIPs attending the annual meeting of the secretive Bilderberg Group were met at Ottawa International Airport by limousine drivers holding signs marked with the single-letter "B." *Ottawa Citizen*, 9 vi 2006, bit.ly/Z56890.

68 This portmanteau-portmanteau describes a range of disproportionately painful self-inflicted wounds:

Burning the roof of your mouth with pizza.[†] ❧ Scalding your tongue testing pasta. ❧ Stubbing your toe. ❧ Skinning your ankle. ❧ Getting a paper cut.[‡] ❧ Biting your tongue. ❧ Clashing your teeth while chewing. Ice cream headache (brain freeze). ❧ Exposing a nail bed. ❧ Blinding yourself with shampoo. ❧ Treading barefoot onto Lego. ❧ Lacerating your fingers on a retracting metal tape measure. (☜8) ❧ Scalding your feet in a hot bath. ❧ Walking into a pane of glass. ❧ Door-slamming a digit. ❧ Slicing a finger while chopping. ❧ Skinning your knuckles while grating. ❧ Touching sensitive parts with chilli-tainted fingers. ❧ Braining yourself while uncorking a bottle. ❧ Flipping an eyelid inside out. ❧ Stepping on the upended tines of a rake.[*] ❧ Kicking what proves to be an immovable object. ❧ Head-butting a door lintel or overhanging branch. ❧ Cutting yourself shaving. ❧ Zapping your funny bone.[§]

[†] See M. L. Dembert & H. S. Faust, "Pizza Palate," *The Journal of the American Dental Association* 109, №2 (Aug 1984): 138.

[‡] "Contrast the paper-cut experience with the experience of individuals who have been stabbed or shot, many of whom first become aware of their injury because of a feeling of warmth on the skin not because of wounded deep tissue." Peggy Mason, *Medical Neurobiology* (Oxford University Press, 2011), 436.
[*] Cf. Robert Frost's "The Objection to Being Stepped On" (1957) – which may have been inspired by his wife, Elinor, who stepped on a rake in 1927, breaking her nose. See N. L. Tuten & J. Zubizarreta, *The Robert Frost Encyclopedia* (Greenwood, 2001), 245.
[§] & ➧ It has been suggested that the funny bone is so called because it is near the humerus. *Kakophonieknochen* derives from the German for "funny bone," *Musikknochen* ("music bone").

◆ ◆ ◆

69 When two women commended Samuel Johnson on expurgating all the "*naughty* words" from his new dictionary, the Great Cham replied: "What! my dears! then you have been looking for them?"[†]

[†] Henry Digby Beste, *Personal and Literary Memorials* (Henry Colburn, 1829), 12.
» Many rude words exist, but only one rude number.

Flughafenbegrüßungsfreude

floog-hah-fen – beh-gruu-soongs – froy-duh

~

Childish delight at being greeted at the airport.

AIRPORT-GREETING-JOY

Kakophonieknochenbruch

kah-koh-fo-nee – k'nocch-en-broocch

~

Minor, yet unreasonably painful, self-inflicted injuries.

CACOPHONY-BONE-FRACTURE

Schmutzwortsuche

shmootz-vohrt – zoo-cche

~

Looking up rude words in the dictionary.

DIRTY-WORD-SEARCH

70 A neurochemical explanation for this sensation was suggested by David G. Myers:

> Savoring that memory of your first kiss requires a mental symphony conductor that retrieves snippets from various cortical storage sites and integrates them with the emotional associations provided by your amygdala.[†]

Sadly, though, the amygdala does not always play ball. Research from 2008 indicated that 66 per cent of women have "dumped a man based on the first kiss."[‡]

[†] David G. Myers, *Psychology*, 7th ed. (Worth, 2004), 360.
[‡] "Make Sure She Invites You Back," *Men's Health*, Jul–Aug 2008, 64. The magazine suggests you "trace her lips with your tongue, and alternate soft kisses with gentle sucking on her lips."
↝ *Haftung* has senses of "liability" and "responsibility," but also "grip," as a car grips the road. It derives from *haften*, which means both "to stick" and "to be responsible (for)."

---

71 An indication of the complexity of post-divorce friendships is given by some of the index headings from the Relate guide *How to Have a Healthy Divorce*:

friends
  effects of divorce
  ex-partner as a friend
  ex-partner's friends
  financial help from
  impacts of your divorce
  maintaining friendships
  support from
friendship goals
friendship map
  after divorce

friendships after divorce
  deepening friendships
  expanding your friendships
  friendship map
  how you would like your
    friendships to be
  nurturing friendships
  re-evaluating
  your intimacy circle[†]

[†] Paula Hall, *How to Have a Healthy Divorce: A Relate Guide* (Vermilion, 2008), 210.
↝ *Scheidungskreidekreisprobe* refers to Bertolt Brecht's *c.*1948 play *Der kaukasische Kreidekreis* (*The Caucasian Chalk Circle*).

---

72 Jean-Paul Sartre cited this urge as an example of "anguish in the face of the future," writing:

> I approach the precipice, and my scrutiny is searching for myself in my very depths. In terms of this moment, I play with my possibilities. My eyes, running over the abyss from top to bottom, imitate the possible fall and realize it symbolically.[†]

A similar phenomenon is occasionally felt by drivers who vaguely prod the idea of "ending it all" with a flick of the steering wheel, but don't.

[†] Jean-Paul Sartre, *Being and Nothingness* (1943), trans. Hazel E. Barnes (Methuen, 1957), 32.
» Dignitas, the Swiss "assisted-suicide centre," reported in 2006 that some 70 per cent of those with a "provisional green light" (i.e., confirmation a doctor would write them a fatal prescription) did not contact the clinic again. Dignitas founder Ludwig Minelli said: "They know, 'I could go through this emergency exit if really I am in difficulties,' and this is calming them." "The Suicide Tourist," *Frontline*, PBS, 22 i 2006, to.pbs.org/cpLJnU.

Lippenhaftung

lip-pen – hahf-toong

⌄

The lingering sensation of a first kiss.

LIP-STICK

Scheidungskreidekreisprobe

shy-doongs – cry-duh-cryss – pro-buh

⌄

The distribution of friends after a divorce.

DIVORCE-CHALK-CIRCLE-TRIAL

Abgrundsanziehung

ahb-groonts – ahn-tsee-oong

⌄

Toying with the (non-suicidal) idea of jumping from a height.

ABYSS-ATTRACTION

73 Since people inevitably apologize for not knowing any jokes, we tend to assume that a memory for jokes is an asset. But is it? Jokes are aggressive beasts, demanding time, attention, and approbation. And joke-telling is an aggressive act. Comedians habitually talk of "killing" and "slaying" their audience, and of "dying" when their routine fails. (Of course, most jokes have a "butt" and all have a "punchline.") As Gershon Legman wrote in his magisterial book *Rationale of the Dirty Joke*:

> The teller of the joke betrays his hidden hostility and signals his victory by being, theoretically at least, the one person present *who does not laugh*.[†]

---

† Gershon Legman, *Rationale of the Dirty Joke: An Analysis of Sexual Humor* (Jonathan Cape, 1968), 9.
↝ *Scherzkeks* ("joke cookie" or "wisecracker") is one of a number of vaguely derogatory terms for those who attempt to be funny. Others include *Spaßvogel* ("funny bird") and its feminine analogue *Ulknudel* ("joke noodle"), and *Witzbold* – suggesting "somebody boldly telling jokes."

74 This irrational, if all-too-human, feeling may have a deeper resonance, according to Rabbi Menachem Mendel Schneerson:

> Because time itself is like a spiral, something special happens on your birthday each year: The same energy that G-d invested in you at birth is present once again. It is our duty to be receptive to that force.[†]

---

† *Toward a Meaningful Life: The Wisdom of the Rebbe Menachem Mendel Schneerson*, adapted by Simon Jacobson (William Morrow, 2002), 18–19.
» A consequence of this sensation is the deflation you experience when others forget your Special Day – as Pooh explained to Piglet: "… poor Eeyore is in a Very Sad Condition, because it's his birthday, and nobody has taken any notice of it, and he's very Gloomy." A. A. Milne, *Winnie-the-Pooh* (1926) (Methuen Children's, 1973), 76.
↝ *Extrawurst* ("bonus sausage") denotes "special treatment" in German; thus, an *Extrawursttag* is a day of special treatment.

75 A recurring theme of the American Dream is that small towns are there to be abandoned in the quest for fortune and fame in the Big City – as celebrated by Fred Ebb's 1977 lyrics for "New York, New York." A contrary opinion has it that small towns offer community and companionship – as well as conditions ideal for observing one's fellow man. It is no accident that Agatha Christie created the village of St Mary Mead as a microcosm from which mischief and evil of every hue could be extrapolated. As Jane Marple explained:

> "Human nature, dear, is very much the same everywhere. It is more difficult to observe it closely in a city, that is all."[†]

---

† Agatha Christie, *They Do It with Mirrors* (Collins, 1952), 16.
» Having lived in Cape Cod for some ten years, the artist Edward Gorey was asked in an interview if he missed New York: "I remember sitting in one of those Greek diners. … I thought, 'There are more people passing this window than Jane Austen saw in her entire life. What good is this doing me?'" Scott Baldauf, "Edward Gorey: Portrait of the Artist in Chilling Color," *The Christian Science Monitor*, 31 x 1996, bit.ly/RyXnT2.

Witzfindungsstörung

vits-fin-doongs – shtoo-roong

~

The inability to remember jokes.

JOKE-FINDING-DYSFUNCTION

Extrawursttagsgefühl

ex-tra-voorst-tahgs – ghe-fuul

~

An irrational sensation of specialness on your birthday.

BONUS-SAUSAGE-DAY-FEELING

Provinztrübsinn

proh-vince – truub-zin

~

The claustrophobia of a small town (that may inspire great things).

LITTLE-TOWN-BLUES

Schattenfreude

76 The term "sleep machismo" is generally credited to the chronobiologist Charles Czeisler, who said, "It amazes me that contemporary work and social culture glorifies sleeplessness in the way we once glorified people who could hold their liquor."[†]

Margaret Thatcher famously glorified sleep machismo. Yet Ferdinand Mount deftly revealed that the "publicly declared dogma that the Iron Lady requires less sleep than other mortals" may have been a sham. Mount describes how, late at night, Thatcher's advisors would excuse themselves, feigning fatigue: "She makes a show of getting down to serious work as we troop off upstairs, but as I turn off the minstrels' gallery towards my room, I catch sight of the little figure down below gathering up her things and going off to bed, her reputation for being indefatigable undented."[‡]

[†] Charles A. Czeisler, "Sleep Deficit: The Performance Killer," *Harvard Business Review* 84, № 10 (Oct 2006): 53–59.
[‡] Ferdinand Mount, *Cold Cream* (Bloomsbury, 2008), 323.
[~] Arianna Huffington tweeted that she prefers the term "braggadozio," 29 iii 2011, bit.ly/11q3XRQ.

77 This portmanteau-portmanteau describes a range of acts of personal grooming and "monkey picking":

Biting your fingernails. ❦ Brushing "sleep" from your eyes. ❦ Cleaning under your nails. ❦ Cracking your knuckles. ❦ Cricking your neck. ❦ Dislodging interdental debris. ❦ Excavating a lump of hardened ear wax. ❦ Exploding pus from a pimple. ❦ Extracting a splinter. ❦ Fingering away grease from the undulations of your outer ear. ❦ Forcing out a blackhead. ❦ Hawking phlegm. ❦ Inspecting your soiled lavatory paper or handkerchief. ❦ Mining a solidified nugget of snot. ❦ Peeling away a perfect arc of toenail. ❦ Picking off a scab or sunburned skin. ❦ Pinching out belly-button fluff. ❦ Plucking eyebrow, ear, or nasal hair. ❦ Probing a sore tooth or under the flap of gum (operculum) covering a wisdom tooth. ❦ Pumicing dead skin. ❦ Pushing back your cuticles. ❦ Rubbing away smegma from the folds of your genitals. ❦ Scraping the white coating off your tongue. ❦ Scratching an itch. ❦ Scouring plaque off your teeth. ❦ Smearing away sweat from under your watchband. ❦ Sniffing snot into your throat. ❦ Tweezing an ingrowing hair. ❦ Uncaking clumps of deodorant from your armpits. ❦ Wiping away "toe jam."

78 The staggering quantity of research into why one yawn provokes another suggests that writing about yawning may be as contagious as yawning itself. Indeed, this subject has been discussed for centuries. Aristotle likened the contagion of yawning among men to the contagion of urination among animals.[†] And Leonardo da Vinci wrote:

> A painter once painted a picture which caused everybody who saw it to yawn, and this happened every time the eye fell on the picture, which represented a person yawning.[‡]

[†] *Pseudo-Aristoteles (Pseudo-Alexander): Supplementa Problematorum*, eds. Sophia Kapetanaki & Robert W. Sharples (Walter de Gruyter, 2006), 147.
[‡] Leonardo da Vinci, *Thoughts on Art and Life*, trans. Maurice Baring (Merrymount Press, 1906), 124.
[»] Perhaps the most celebrated painting of a yawn is a self-portrait by Joseph Ducreux, who depicted himself mouth agape, back arched, arm outstretched, in delicious pandiculation.
[~] *Gähnverseuchung* is formed from *gähnen* ("to yawn") and *Genverseuchung* ("genetic contamination").

Schlafchauvi

shlahf – shoh-vee

~

One who takes pride in getting little sleep.

SLEEP-MACHO

23, 30

Popelplaisir

poh-pel – pleh-zeer

~

Intimate moments of personal grooming.

BOGEY-BLISS

Gähnverseuchung

ghehn – fair-zoy-cchoong

~

One yawn's irrestrainable power to provoke another.

YAWN-CONTAMINATION

79 In May 2013, the fifth edition of the American Psychiatric Association's *Diagnostic and Statistical Manual of Mental Disorders* (DSM-5) promoted hoarding from a subtype of Obsessive-Compulsive Disorder, or Obsessive-Compulsive Personality Disorder, to a distinct diagnosis, with the title bump: "Hoarding Disorder."

➤ "Plyushkin syndrome" is a Russian equivalent of the West's "hoarding disorder" or "senile squalor syndrome." It is named after the character created by Nikolai Gogol in his celebrated 1842 novel *Dead Souls*. Plyushkin is a rich but miserly landowner who rejects human company as he obsessively collects useless objects. (Of course, there are a number of notable literary hoarders, not least Miss Havisham from *Great Expectations*.) The animal most associated with hoarding in Germany is not the squirrel, but the hamster; indeed, *hamstern* means "to hoard." A range of other German compounds refer to rodents of the subfamily Cricetinae, for example: *Hamsterkauf* ("hamster purchase") means "panic buying," and *Hamsterfahrt* ("hamster trip") refers to the practice of urbanites journeying into the countryside to stock up on food after World War II.

80 In *The Pleasures of Cooking for One*, the celebrated editor Judith Jones elegantly defended cooking alone:

> If you like good food, why not honor yourself enough to make a pleasing meal and relish every mouthful? Of course, we want to share with others, too, but we don't always have family and friends around. And I can't see taking in my neighbors every night.[†]

However, John le Carré's cuckolded über-spy, George Smiley, offered a more jaundiced view:

> Anywhere else in the house – even in bed – you can cut yourself off, read your books, deceive yourself that solitude is best. But in the kitchen the signs of incompleteness are too strident.[‡]

---

† Judith Jones, *The Pleasures of Cooking for One* (Knopf, 2009), ix.
‡ John le Carré, *Smiley's People* (1979) (Scribner, 2008), 87.
➤ *Einsiedelei* is a slightly archaic word for "hermitage"; *sieden* means "to boil."

81

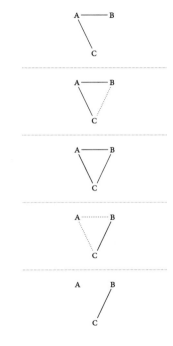

Pljuschkinhamster

plyoosh-kin – hahm-ster

The urge to hoard.

PLYUSHKIN'S HAMSTER

🐌 66

Einsiedelei

ine-zee-duh-lie

The melancholy of cooking for one.

LONELY-KETTLE

🐌 22, 71

Dreiecksumgleichung

dry-ex – oom-gly-cchoong

When two friends you've introduced form a new friendship that excludes you.

TRIANGLE-REORGANIZATION

82 Some of those with rare blood types enjoy being unusual;[†] some relish doing good (☞ 91); and some are banking on reciprocity. Christopher Hitchens explained why he donated his "exclusive corpuscles":[‡]

> When I give blood … I do not lose a pint, but someone else gains one. There is something about this that appeals to me, and I derive other satisfactions as well from being of assistance to a fellow creature. Furthermore, I have a very rare blood type and I hope very much that when I am in need of a transfusion someone else will have thought and acted in precisely the same way.[*]

[†] Related to this is the perverse pride with which some people tell doctors that they are allergic to vital drugs, such as penicillin.
[‡] Christopher Hitchens, "The Vietnam Syndrome," *Vanity Fair*, Aug 2006, 128.
[*] Christopher Hitchens, *The Portable Atheist* (Da Capo Press, 2007), xvi–xvii.
[↝] *Blutarmut* ("anaemia") is literally "blood poverty."

83 The travel site TripAdvisor has more than 26,000 reviews mentioning "food poisoning,"[†] many of which illustrate that people know just what made them sick:

> got food poisoning from their "Tasmanian salmon". Spent the night throwing up and diarrhoea, followed by 10 hours on an iv drip. Do not go.

> I puked for several hours after I ate the prairie fire roll and white dynamic roll.

> Staff was friendly but pork gave me vile food poisoning.

> Please God avoid the crab and shellfish, I have had two days bad food poisoning so far.

> Gritty mushrooms on a pizza left us hugging our toilet.

> We think it was the potato salad.

[†] 26,239 at the time of writing; bit.ly/ZYim1d.
[»] In *Monty Python's The Meaning of Life* (1983), the Grim Reaper reveals to his dinner party victims that it was … *the salmon mousse.*

84 Describing the hallucinatory sense of battle, and indeed of being shot, Norman Mailer wrote:

> It seemed unreal, the way a man's face may sometimes seem unreal if he gazes at it too long in the mirror.[†]

Antoine Roquentin, the protagonist in Jean-Paul Sartre's novel *Nausea*, added this evolutionary detail:

> When I was little, my Aunt Bigeois told me "If you look at yourself too long in the mirror, you'll see a monkey." I must have looked at myself even longer than that: what I see is well below the monkey, on the fringe of the vegetable world, at the level of jellyfish.[‡]

[†] Norman Mailer, *The Naked and the Dead* (1948) (Owl Books, 1998), 355.
[‡] Jean-Paul Sartre, *Nausea* (1938), trans. Lloyd Alexander (New Directions, 1964), 16–17.

82

Bluthochmut

bloot – hohcch-moot

~

The pride some people take in having a rare blood type.

BLOOD-HAUGHTINESS

83

Bauchgefühlbauchgefühl

baucch-ghe-fuul – baucch-ghe-fuul

~

Instinctively knowing what gave you food poisoning.

GUT FEELING GUT FEELING

84

Spiegelbildauflösung

shpee-ghel-bilt – aowf-loo-zoong

~

Staring into a mirror until you begin not to recognize your own face.

REFLECTION-DISINTEGRATION

Schadenfreude

85 Much has been written on the shock and denial of a life-changing medical diagnosis. But many lives are exploded by a moment of *personal* medical discovery – about either oneself (feeling a lump, finding blood) or someone close (observing a tremor, noticing confusion). Even if such discoveries await the imprimatur of formal medicine, they encapsulate the fearful knowledge that once a certain Rubicon of health is crossed, the next river to be confronted is the Styx.

» In some cases, our first external symptoms are merely the tip of an internal iceberg. For example, in Parkinson's disease, 60–70 per cent of the brain's dopamine-producing cells will already have been lost before the characteristic tremor, and other movement disturbances, become apparent. See Niall P. Quinn et al., "Movement Disorders," *Neurology: A Queen Square Textbook*, eds. C. Clarke, R. Howard, M. Rossor, & S. Shorvon (Wiley-Blackwell, 2009), 157.
↜ In Greek mythology, Erebus (Darkness) is the son of Chaos; Erebus is also a place of cavernous gloom between the earth and the underworld through which the dead must pass.

86 "Few things are as uncomfortable as being in the presence of a couple that is openly fighting, bickering, or putting each other down," observed the sociologist David Newman.† Yet pleasure (*Schadenfreude?*) clearly exists in watching others argue, when at a safe distance. In her remarkable discussion of movies and marriage, Jeanine Basinger noted that in the "studio system" era,

"bicker" was a language all Americans spoke. Any movie married people who did not bicker had limited screen time as a couple. One of them was going to die very, very soon, or be shoved aside while the other invented something useful.‡

The ascendancy of confessional and "reality" television suggests that "screwball comedy" has merely devolved into oddball tragedy.

† David M. Newman, *Sociology: Exploring the Architecture of Everyday Life*, 7th ed. (Pine Forge Press, 2008), 173.
‡ Jeanine Basinger, *I Do and I Don't: A History of Marriage in the Movies* (Borzoi, 2012), 83.

87 Karl Marx argued that money has the power to "transform all my incapacities into their contrary":

I am ugly, but I can buy for myself the most *beautiful* of women. Therefore I am not *ugly*, for the effect of *ugliness* – its deterrent power – is nullified by money.†

Groucho Marx chipped in:

I know this sordid discussion of money hasn't much to do with sex, but just try to take a girl out when you're broke and see how far you get.‡

† Karl Marx, "The Power of Money in Bourgeois Society," in *The Marx-Engels Reader*, ed. R. Tucker (W. W. Norton, 1978), 103–04.
‡ Groucho Marx, *Memoirs of a Mangy Lover* (B. Geis, 1963), 66.
↜ Deutschmarks were in circulation between 1948 and 2001/02.

85
☞ 110

Erebusterror

eh-reh-booss – tehr-rohr

~

Dread at the first indications of a fatal disease.

EREBUS-TERROR

86
☞ 107

Ringrichterscham

ring-ricch-ter – shahm

~

Embarrassment at being present when a couple argue.

BOXING-REFEREE-SHAME

87

Marksismus

mahr-kseez-moose

~

The distorting influence of wealth.

[DEUTSCH]MARKS-ISM

Schottenfreude

88 In 2012, global teen pop sensation Justin Bieber confirmed that some of his fans (the "Beliebers") had nicknamed his manhood "Jerry."[†] Those anxious for a more literary precedent before naming their genitalia might take comfort in the work of D. H. Lawrence:

> "Do you know what I thought?" she said
> suddenly. "It suddenly came to me. You are
> the 'Knight of the Burning Pestle.'"
> "Ay! And you? Are you the Lady of the Red-hot
> Mortar?"
> "Yes!" she said. "Yes! You're Sir Pestle and I'm
> Lady Mortar."
> "All right – then I'm knighted. John Thomas is
> Sir John, to your Lady Jane."[‡]

[†] Justin Bieber, interviewed by James Barr on the London radio station Capital FM, 24 iv 2012, bit.ly/Io3zYl. Bieber jokingly added, "My fans are kinda inappropriate, but it's funny."
[‡] Lawrence, op. cit., 227.
↝ *Verniedlichung* means "belittlement," but with a sense of being cutely diminutive; *Schniedel* is slang for the *membrum virile*.

89 This portmanteau-portmanteau describes a range of curiously unpleasant sensations, for example:

Warm lavatory seats. ❦ Wet lavatory seats. ❦ Greasy telephone receivers. ❦ Open-mouth kisses from relative strangers. ❦ Putting on communal bowling shoes. ❦ Fingering communal bowling balls. ❦ Soiled banknotes. ❦ Under-seat chewing gum.[†] ❦ Gritty lettuce. ❦ Fetid clothes left in the washing machine. ❦ Mouth breathing.[‡] ❦ Water-fountain paranoia. ❦ Sticky library books. ❦ Overlong handshakes. ❦ Dead-fish handshakes. ❦ Fingertip-only handshakes. ❦ Moist shoelace ends. ❦ Writing with a pencil chewed by someone else. ❦ Hotel room TV remotes. ❦ Chewing eggshell. ❦ Hair in food. ❦ Cold, damp bedsheets.[*] ❦ Dog-eared waiting room magazines. ❦ Unwrapped restaurant mints. ❦ Containers pooled with soupy water after a dishwasher cycle has ended. ❦ Vile telephone kiosks. ❦ Stagnant flower water. ❦ Wet coins in change. ❦ Shiny fabric head- or armrests. ❦ Unripe avocados softened by customer handling. ❦ Murky swimming pool footbaths. ❦ Watery breakfast-buffet eggs. ❦ Pubic-hairy soap. ❦ Puddle-sodden socks. ❦ Limp and faded salad bars. ❦ Soap-tray gunk. ❦ Encountering an unflushed toilet.[§]

[†] In 1948, during the Berlin Airlift, Bob Hope joked, "Yesterday a B-39 flew in a hundred tons of chewing gum … and right behind it was a plane with a load of theatre seats to stick it under." W. R. Faith, *Bob Hope: A Life in Comedy* (Da Capo Press, 2009), 194.
[‡] See Clinton Wagner, *Habitual Mouth-Breathing: Its Causes, Effects, and Treatment* (G. P. Putnam's Sons, 1881).
[*] According to Mrs Mary Eaton, "Persons who keep [damp beds] in their houses are guilty of a species of murder, though it unfortunately happens that no housewife is willing to acknowledge that *her* beds were ever damp." *The Cook and Housekeeper's Complete and Universal Dictionary* (J. & R. Childs, 1822), 104.
[§] "–Bog's fuckin blocked, mate. Ye'll no be able tae shite in that. He gestures tae the seatless bowl fall ay broon water, toilet paper and lumps ay floating shite." Irvine Welsh, *Trainspotting* (Secker & Warburg, 1993), 24.

◆　　◆　　◆

90 This phenomenon is akin to feeling that: removed spectacles are still on your nose; earplugs are still in your ears; a pill or bolus of food is still in your oesophagus; or a (Christmas paper) hat is still on your head. (The opposite of this might be the sensations felt when your feet first touch the floor after a prolonged period of time in [a hospital] bed.)

88

Verschniedlichung

fair-shneed-lih-cchoong

~

Bestowing nicknames on your sexual parts, or those parts of a loved one.

"BEWILLIEMENT"

89

Bähgriff

beh-griff

~

Everyday experiences that prompt you to recoil with various degrees of repugnance.

DISGUSTING-IDEA

90

Mundphantom

moondt – fahn-tohm

~

Feeling that the thermometer is still under your tongue after it's been removed.

MOUTH-PHANTOM

Schottenfreude

91 This portmanteau-portmanteau describes those minor (yet oddly pride-burnishing) acts of civic duty:

Telling someone the time. ❦ Giving directions.† ❦ Holding a door. (☞ 104) ❦ Helping someone across the street. ❦ Allowing someone (back) into line. ❦ Pulling over for emergency vehicles.‡ ❦ Asking "Which floor?" and pressing the appropriate button. ❦ Comforting a stranger. ❦ Waving a vehicle forward. ❦ Offering to take a photograph. ❦ Handing in lost property. ❦ Lifting a pushchair up or down stairs. ❦ Volunteering your seat. ❦ Pushing a broken-down car.* ❦ Signing for a neighbour's delivery. ❦ Assisting someone who has fallen. ❦ Carrying someone's bags. ❦ Delaying a bus so another passenger can reach it in time. ❦ Swapping seats so a couple can sit together. ❦ Giving hand signals to a driver making a tricky manoeuvre. ❦ Offering your arm to the blind. ❦ Tipping like Sinatra. ❦ Briefly guarding someone's belongings. ❦ Flashing your headlights to alert another driver that his headlights are off. § ❦ Admitting you've been given too much change. ❦ Clearing snow from the path of an infirm neighbour. ❦ Coming forward as a witness. ❦ Dialling 999. ❦ Donating blood. (☏ 82) ❦ Witnessing a legal document.

† Although John Irving wrote: "We don't enjoy giving directions in New Hampshire – we tend to think that if you don't know where you're going, you don't belong where you are." *A Prayer for Owen Meany* (Ballantine Books, 1989), 16–17.

‡ "One of the triumphs of civilization, Peter Walsh thought. … Every cart or carriage of its own accord drew aside to let the ambulance pass." Virginia Woolf, *Mrs Dalloway* (1925) (Oxford University Press, 2000), 128.

* In 1970, Italy's highest civil court ruled that only qualified drivers could push broken-down cars. Offenders risked a $64 fine, or 6 months in jail. *Spokane Daily Chronicle*, 30 xii 1970, 1.

§ Or that her lights are on full beam; or that there is a speed trap ahead; or to salute one driving the same (unusual) model of car; or to tell an overtaking artic that its back wheels have passed you.

◆　◆　◆

92 Konrad Duden was one of Germany's foremost lexicographers. In 1880, he issued *Vollständiges Orthographisches Wörterbuch der deutschen Sprache* (Complete Orthographical Dictionary of the German Language). The various Duden dictionaries still published remain key German reference texts. (In 1991, a main-belt asteroid was named after Konrad Duden: 26119 DUDEN [1991 TN7].)

93 In *The Mezzanine*, Nicholson Baker explored the problem some people have with "relaxing their uriniferous tubing," and suggested a cure. When flanked by someone with no problem peeing, but yourself frozen:

Imagine yourself turning and dispassionately urinating onto the side of his head. Imagine your voluminous stream making fleeting parts in his hair.†

† Baker, *The Mezzanine*, op. cit., 84.

≫ In 1954, Williams and Degenhardt proposed a clinical term for this condition – *paruresis* – and defined it as "a functional disorder of micturition characterized by psychosomatic symptomatology that involves an inability to void urine in public facilities." G. W. Williams & E. T. Degenhardt, "Paruresis: A Survey of a Disorder of Micturition," *The Journal of General Psychology* 51 (1954): 19–29.

↝ *Zurückhaltung* (literally "holding back") has senses of both "modesty" and "retention."

Sozialpflichterfüllungsstolz

zo-tsee-ahl-pfliccht – air-fuu-loongs – shtolts

˄

The satisfaction you feel after performing minor acts of altruistic civic duty.

SOCIAL-DUTY-COMPLETION-PRIDE

Dudenblitz

doo-den – blitz

˄

Thinking of the perfect word just as you reach for the thesaurus.

DUDEN-FLASH

Pissoirzurückhaltung

piss-swar – tsoo-ruuk-hahl-toong

˄

Inability to urinate when other people are present.

URINAL-RETENTION

94 Cornelia Otis Skinner called this the "where-to-look" problem, and observed that it occurs in a range of situations, from elevators to railway dining cars:

> The inevitable moment when glances meet but they meet only to shoot instantly away.[†]

Alexander Solzhenitsyn described a procedure in the Lubyanka prison's corridors, where guards "clicked" their tongues, as if calling a dog, to signal they had a prisoner under escort. A clicking guard listened out for the clicks of other guards, and would force his prisoner into a tiny cell to prevent captives from meeting:

> One prisoner must never be allowed to encounter another, never be allowed to draw comfort or support from the look in his eyes.[‡]

[†] Cornelia Otis Skinner, "Where to Look," *Bottoms Up!* (Dodd, Mead, 1955), 31.
[‡] Alexander Solzhenitsyn, *The First Circle* (1968), trans. Michael Guybon (Fontana, 1971), 658–59.
➤ Nystagmus involves rapid, uncontrollable eye movements.

95

➤ *Hochkommakrankheit* is "high comma (i.e., apostrophe) disease."

96 There is, inevitably, a small but enthusiastic knot of scientific research into the "broken escalator phenomenon"[†] – the psychological effect of which was brilliantly illustrated by Augusten Burroughs:

> The escalator is broken, and the disappointment starts sinking from your chest, gathering mass along the way until it hits your feet, where it congeals and leaves you with twenty-pound heels.[‡]

[†] See, for example, R. F. Reynolds & A. M. Bronstein, "The Broken Escalator Phenomenon," *Experimental Brain Research* 151, № 3 (Aug 2003): 301–08; and K. L. Bunday et al., "The Effect of Trial Number on the Emergence of the 'Broken Escalator' Locomotor Aftereffect," *Experimental Brain Research* 174, № 2 (Sep 2006): 270–78. Marvellously, this field of inquiry employs terms such as "forward trunk overshoot on gait termination."
[‡] Augusten Burroughs, "Up the Escalator," in *Magical Thinking: True Stories* (St. Martin's Press, 2004), 260.
➤ *Rolltreppe* ("rolling stairs") is German for "escalator."

94
☞ 104

Dielennystagmus

dee-len – nooss-tahg-moose

~

Repeatedly catching and avoiding people's gazes when, say, approaching them down a long corridor.

HALLWAY-NYSTAGMUS

95

Hochkommakrankheit

hohcch-kohm-ma – crahnk-hite

~

A (banal) obsession with (or general confusion about) (the deployment of) apostrophes.

APOSTROPHITIS

96

Rollschleppe

rohl-shlep-puh

~

The exhausting trudge up a stationary escalator.

ESCALATOR-SCHLEP

97 Elisabeth Bednar, who calls herself "disfigured from birth," affectingly described how it feels to be the subject of barely concealed curiosity and judgement:

> There is the initial stare, then the look away, before a second, furtive glance inevitably puts the beheld immediately in a separate class.[†]

---

† Elisabeth A. Bednar, "Self-Help for the Facially Disfigured: Commentary on the 'Quasimodo Complex,'" in *The Tyranny of the Normal: An Anthology*, eds. Carol Donley & Sheryl Buckley (Kent State University Press, 1996), 53.

» A (melo)dramatic account of our inability to look at physical deformity with a steady eye was reported by F. C. Carr-Gomm, Chairman of the London Hospital. On 30 xi 1886, Mr Carr-Gomm wrote to *The Times* to solicit public funds for the care of Mr Joseph Merrick, whose appearance was "so terrible indeed that women and nervous persons fly in terror from the sight of him." (Joseph Merrick is also known as the "Elephant Man.")

» A corollary of this is "koinophilia," whereby people are attracted to those with "average" features.

➛ *Leid* has senses of "sorrow," "harm," and "misfortune."

98 This English phrase was coined by Alan Bennett, in his January 21, 1980, diary entry on the death of the writer, photographer, and designer Cecil Beaton:

> The obituaries mention his capacity for hard work but not his toughness. The toughness of the dandy.[†]

Few have personified this as publicly as Quentin Crisp:

> As my appearance progressed from the effeminate to the bizarre, the reaction of strangers passed from startled contempt to outraged hatred.

Despite strangers jeering and assaulting him, Crisp remained unbowed: "I was not frightened. Because I still believed that I could educate them, I was happy."[‡]

---

† Alan Bennett, *Writing Home* (Picador, 2003), 135.

‡ Quentin Crisp, *The Naked Civil Servant* (1968) (Penguin, 1997), 44.

➛ *Schnauze* is an animal's muzzle, i.e., its nose, mouth, and jaw.

99 "Nothing is more hopeless than a scheme of merriment. … The jest which is expected is already destroyed," thundered Samuel Johnson,[†] who would doubtless have agreed with whoever nicknamed New Year's Eve "the Nuremberg of the fun fascists." ❦ In a delightful analysis of "organized fun" in the workplace, Sam Warren and Stephen Fineman explained that, while fun and laughter inevitably exist within some social and cultural conventions,

> where fun is "required" and its structure imposed, where it is heavily "managed," the frisson of self-authorship and surprise are lost; feelings of fun are muted, heavily bounded or effectively extinguished. In these circumstances people may still laugh and smile, but hollowed of any feelings of pleasure.[‡]

---

† Samuel Johnson, *The Idler* № 58 (26 v 1759).

‡ Sam Warren & Stephen Fineman, "Ambivalence and Paradox in a 'Fun' Work Environment," in *Humour, Work and Organization*, eds. Robert Westwood & Carl Rhodes (Routledge, 2007), 106.

➛ As the Germans say: *Spaß muss sein!* ("Fun is a must!").

Blickleid

blick-lide

~

Sneaking sly looks at the physically disabled.

GLANCE-HARM

Schmetterlingsschnauze

shmet-ter-lings – shnaow-tsuh

~

"The toughness of the dandy."

BUTTERFLY-JAWS

Frohsinnsfaschismus

froh-zins – fah-shis-moose

~

The god-awful mediocrity of organized fun.

CHEERFULNESS-FASCISM

Schottenfreude

100 Few writers have described sleep as evocatively as Marcel Proust. The opening pages of *Remembrance of Things Past* are a hymn to the fugue-like state of slumbering, and the "stupid moment of waking":

> When a man is asleep, he has in a circle round him the chain of the hours, the sequence of the years, the order of the heavenly host. Instinctively, when he awakes, he looks to these, and in an instant reads off his own position on the earth's surface and the amount of time that has elapsed during his slumbers; but this ordered procession is apt to grow confused, and to break its ranks.[†]

Inevitably, such confusion will be exacerbated by waking in a bed other than your own – which may explain why Casanova "had a cardinal principle never to sleep in a strange bed."[‡] (Clearly, this didn't cramp his style.)

Petrarch, who was something of a "wandering scholar" (and has been called "the first tourist"), declared, "It is a strange madness, this desire to be for ever sleeping in a strange bed."[*] If this madness exists, it extends to a range of superstitions associated with waking under unfamiliar covers. According to the normally reliable *Gypsy Witch Fortune Teller*, drinking salt water before sleeping will precipitate a thirst that will "cause you to dream; which joined to a strange bed, will have a true effect."[§] Another source noted that maidens desirous of divining a new lover would "in years past" wrap their garter nine times around the post of a strange bed, tying nine knots and incanting these lines:

> This knot I knit, this knot I tie,
> To see my lover as he goes by,
> In his apparel and array,
> As he walks in every day.[‡]

Perhaps because we intuit that any disorientation we feel on waking will be fleeting (like, say, a "dead arm"), it is not especially frightening. As Jack Kerouac wrote:

> I looked at the cracked high ceiling and really didn't know who I was for about fifteen strange seconds. I wasn't scared; I was just somebody else, some stranger, and my whole life was a haunted life, the life of a ghost.[∴]

Indeed, the U.S. Poet Laureate Billy Collins observed:

> When you wake up in a strange bed, often you don't know where you are for a couple of seconds. Surely, that is not a pleasure for everyone, but it is for some. How refreshing to take a little break from always knowing where we are, or least fooling ourselves into thinking so.[ː]

† Marcel Proust, *Remembrance of Things Past*, vol. 1, *Swann's Way* (1913), trans. C. K. Scott Moncrieff (Henry Holt, 1922), 9; 3–4.

‡ Iwan Bloch, *Marquis de Sade: His Life and Works* (1899), trans. James Bruce (Brittany Press, 1948), 114.

* Helen Waddell, *The Wandering Scholars of the Middle Ages* (Constable, 1927), 177.

§ C. B. Case, *Gypsy Witch Fortune Teller* (Shrewsbury, 1930), 141.

‡ T. F. Thiselton-Dyer, *Folk-lore of Women* (McClurg, 1906), 222.

∴ Jack Kerouac, *On the Road* (1957) (Penguin, 2003), 15.

ː Arlo Haskell, "The Pleasures of Disorientation: A Conversation with Billy Collins," Key West Literary Seminar, 20 viii 2009, bit.ly/ZgBXc3.

➤ *Bett* ("bed"); *Trug* ("deceit"); *Betrug* ("fraud" or "cheating").

Betttrug

bett-troog

~

The fleeting sense of disorientation on waking in a strange bed.

BED-DECEPTION

Arztentköstigung

ahrtst – ent-kooss-tee-goong

~

Wherein what the doctor orders you to abstain from are the things you most love.

DOCTOR'S-RATIONS

Straußmanöver

shtraowss – mah-noo-vehr

~

The short-term defence strategy of simply denying reality.

OSTRICH-MANOEUVRE

103 The humorist Stephen Potter wrote: "A good general rule is to state that the bouquet is better than the taste, and vice versa."† ❦ An odd tale of wine tasting is told by Sancho Panza in *Don Quixote*; he claimed: "I have had in my family, by the father's side, two of the rarest tasters that were ever known in La Mancha." Given a hogshead of wine to assess, one man tasted it with the tip of his tongue, the other merely sniffed it:

> The first said the wine savoured of iron; the second said it had rather a twang of goat's leather. The owner protested that the vessel was clean, and the wine neat, so that it could not taste either of iron or leather. Notwithstanding this, the two famous tasters stood positively to what they had said. Time went on; the wine was sold off, and, on cleaning the cask, a small key, hanging to a leathern thong, was found at the bottom.‡

† Stephen Potter, *One-upmanship* (Holt, 1952), 153.
‡ Miguel de Cervantes, *Adventures of Don Quixote de la Mancha* (1605), trans. Charles Jarvis (George Routledge, 1856), 332.

104 This portmanteau-portmanteau describes those predicaments for which there is no polite escape, e.g.:

> Whether to wait for a single penny in change (miserly cheapness) or leave without it (Duke-like condescension).
>
> Whether to hold a door for someone walking a little way behind you (compelling her to speed up) or let it close (in her face).
>
> Whether to inform someone he has halitosis (mortifying) or leave him unaware (cruel).
>
> Whether to ask someone to repeat something for a third time (unthinkable) or pretend you understand (absurd).

➛ *Clashsyndrom* derives from the punk classic "Should I Stay or Should I Go?" – written mainly by Mick Jones for The Clash's 1982 album *Combat Rock*. On its re-release in 1991, to coincide with a Levi's jeans advert in which it was featured, the single hit #14 in the German charts (#16 in Bavaria). See bit.ly/10209nS.

105 Among climbers, the tendency to recklessness when close to a peak is known as "summit fever," and is cautioned against in the adage: "There are old climbers and bold climbers, but no old, bold climbers."

In an analysis of avalanche deaths, Fredston et al. proposed a menagerie of risky climbing behaviour:†

Sheep syndrome............. *blindly following the leader*
Horse syndrome........... *a rush to get back to the barn*
Lion syndrome .. *a rush for "first tracks" (summit fever)*

† J. Fredston, D. Fesler, & B. Tremper, "The Human Factor – Lessons for Avalanche Education," presented at the International Snow Science Workshop, Snowbird, Utah, 1994.
» Related is "VIP passenger syndrome," where pilots make reckless decisions when flying VIPs. It may have been a factor in the plane crash that killed the Polish president, and 95 others, in 2010.
➛ *Watzmannwahn* is named for the Watzmann – the highest peak entirely within Germany, near Berchtesgaden, Bavaria. This 8,900-foot peak and the lesser peaks that flank it are said to personify King Watzmann, his wife, and their various children, who were all petrified as punishment for the king's oppression.

Besserwinzer

bess-ser – vints-er

One of those people who pretend to know more about wine than they do.

KNOW-IT-ALL-VINTNER

Clashsyndrom

klahsh – zoon-drohm

Moments of etiquette perplexity when there is no polite way of behaving.

CLASH-SYNDROME

Watzmannwahn

vahtz-mahn – vahn

The impulse to take impetuous risks when tantalizingly close to your goal.

WATZMANN-DELUSION

Schattenfreude

106 A bovine quintet[†] might come in handy if …

An innocuous remark causes grave offence.[‡] ❧ You find yourself defending a belief you don't hold. ❧ Your interlocutor assumes you share his vile opinions. ❧ Your interlocutor is clearly rehearsing what he will later tell his analyst. ❧ Your conversational thunder is stolen. ❧ You're repeatedly trumped by insistent one-upmanship. ❧ You pretend not to have heard a story.[*] ❧ You're interrupted mid-anecdote. ❧ It's the *other* twin. ❧ You wait patiently for someone to finish a story, so you can tell yours.[§] ❧ One of "your" facts is deployed against you. ❧ You dance the backward-bad-breath-tango. ❧ You mistake a paunch for pregnancy. ❧ You're seated next to someone you've just talked to at length. (☞ 45) ❧ You exhaust your meagre stock of a foreign language. ❧ Both of your neighbours "turn," leaving you to stare at your plate.[‡] ❧ Conversation just dies.[∴] ❧ A lighthearted interjection is met with silence.[⫶] ❧ You suffer the mangling of a joke you would have told better. ❧ You suddenly become aware of your social class. ❧ A lull in ambient noise exposes you as shouting.[⊛] ❧ You babble to fill an awkward silence.[Ħ] ❧ You unwittingly bad-mouth someone to a friend of hers.

† We learn from Honoré de Balzac that the Polish had a phrase for when someone blunders in conversation: "'Harness five bullocks to your cart!' probably because you will need them all to pull you out of the quagmire into which a false step has plunged you." *Old Goriot* (1835), trans. Ellen Marriage (J. M. Dent, 1913), 73.
‡ It is said that one of the architects of Vienna's State Opera house killed himself in 1868, after Emperor Franz Joseph mildly criticized the design. So shocked was the emperor by the consequence of his casual remark, he thereafter restricted his public opinion to: *"Es war sehr schön, es hat mich sehr gefreut"* ("It was very beautiful, I enjoyed it very much"). William M. Johnston, *The Austrian Mind* (1972) (University of California Press, 1983), 175–76.
* After *twice* reassuring Henry Irving that he had not heard the story Irving was telling, Mark Twain ran out of patience: "I can lie once, I can lie twice for courtesy's sake, but I cannot lie three times. I not only heard the story, I wrote it." *The Wit and Wisdom of Mark Twain*, ed. Alex Ayres (1987) (Perennial, 2005), 124.
§ "There is no such thing as conversation. It is an illusion. There are intersecting monologues, that is all." Rebecca West, "There Is No Conversation," *The Harsh Voice* (Doubleday, Doran, 1935), 67.
‡ Hostesses used to "turn the table" during a meal, swapping conversational partners and obliging others to follow suit. See *Amy Vanderbilt's Etiquette* (Doubleday, 1972), 324.
∴ At which the French say, *"Un ange passe"* ("An angel passes").

⫶ "'If the Queen ever feels affronted about something, she has the perfect answer,' explains [the historian] Kenneth Rose. 'She just stares at the person with open eyes, absolutely no expression.'" Robert Hardman, *Her Majesty: Queen Elizabeth II and Her Court* (Pegasus, 2012), eBook.
⊛ The actress Ruth Chatterton found volume an issue when the "talkies" came in: "The microphone fascinates me. Sometimes I talk in my ordinary tones, and they tell me that I am talking too loud. Another time I scream and they tell me to talk louder." Eve Golden, *John Gilbert: The Last of the Silent Film Stars* (University Press of Kentucky, 2013), 188.
Ħ In Western Apache culture, "strangers who are quick to launch into conversation are frequently eyed with undisguised suspicion. A typical reaction to such individuals is that they 'want something,' that is, their willingness to violate convention is attributed to some urgent need which is likely to result in requests for money, labor, or transportation. Another common reaction to talkative strangers is that they are drunk." Keith H. Basso, "'To Give Up on Words': Silence in Western Apache Culture," *Southwestern Journal of Anthropology* 26, № 3 (1970), 213–30.

◆   ◆   ◆

107 I.e., the flexor digitorum longus.

Gesprächsgemetzel

ghe-shprehcchs – ghe-mets-el

~

Moments when, for no good reason, a conversation suddenly goes awry.

CONVERSATION-CARNAGE

Fußfaust

fooss-foust

~

Instinctively curling up your toes in mortification at someone else's embarrassment.

FOOT-FIST

Erlösungsfreudeschuldbewusstsein

air-loo-zoongs – froy-duh – shoold-beh-voost-zyne

~

Guilt at the relief of a loved one's death.

DELIVERANCE-JOY-SHAME

Schottenfreude

109 "Do you seek the most amazing evidence of how far the transfiguring power of ecstasy extends?" asked Friedrich Nietzsche, archly:

"Love" is the evidence: that which is termed love in every language and every speechlessness of the world. Ecstasy contends with reality in such a way that in the consciousness of a lover the original cause is erased and something else seems to appear in its place – a shivering and shining of all the enchanted mirrors of Circe.[†]

The Tamils have a word for this ecstasy – *mayakkam* – which melds the emotions of "dizziness, confusion, intoxication, [and] delusion."[‡]

† Friedrich Nietzsche, *Werke: Der Wille zur Macht* [*The Will to Power*] (1884–88) (C.G. Naumann, 1906), 63. In Greek mythology, Circe, the daughter of Helios, was the sorceress of the island of Aeaea who transformed some of Odysseus's men into pigs.
‡ Margaret Trawick, *Notes on Love in a Tamil Family* (1990) (University of California Press, 1992), 113–14.

110 This portmanteau-portmanteau describes some of the enlightening aspects of chronic and acute illness:

The relief of surrendering yourself to medical care. ❦ "How few of his friends' houses would a man choose to be at, when he is sick!"[†] ❦ Surprise at whom you do (and don't) turn to for help. ❦ Perspective.[†] ❦ The distraction of waiting for test results. ❦ The unevenness of progress.[*] ❦ The fear of relapse. ❦ The despondency of night; the relief of dawn.[§] ❦ Irrationally wanting your doctor to have had your disease. ❦ Irrationally being reassured that celebrities have your disease. ❦ The necessity of being a vigilant patient.[‡] ❦ The anticlimax of telling people your illness isn't cancer.[∴] ❦ "It is only when the rich are sick, that they fully feel the impotence of wealth."[‡] ❦ How the culture you can tolerate is a barometer of recovery.[⊛] ❦ The tendency to solipsism.[¤]

† Samuel Johnson, quoted in Boswell, *The Life* ..., op. cit., 486.
‡ "Introduce into the chamber of a sick and dying man the whole pantheon of idols, which he has vainly worshipped – fame, wealth, pleasure, beauty, power. What miserable comforters are they all!" Rev. Joseph S. Buckminster, *Sermons* (John Eliot, 1814), 49.

* "Recovery was not to be seen as a smooth slope, but as a series of radical steps, each inconceivable, impossible, from the step below." Oliver Sacks, *A Leg to Stand On* (Touchstone, 1998), 125.
§ "For what human ill does not dawn seem to be an alleviation?" Thornton Wilder, *The Bridge of San Luis Rey* (Grosset & Dunlap, 1927), 119. ❦ Marcel Proust described an invalid who, waking in a strange hotel, is delighted to see "daylight shewing under his bedroom door," as morning will bring help. His hopes are dashed when the midnight gaslight is snuffed. *Swann's Way*, op. cit., 2.
‡ "The patient must combat the disease along with the physician." *The Genuine Works of Hippocrates*, trans. Francis Adams (William Wood, 1886), vol. 1, 300.
∴ "While there are several chronic diseases more destructive to life than cancer, none is more feared." Charles H. Mayo & William A. Hendricks, "Carcinoma of the Right Segment of the Colon," *Annals of Surgery* 83, № 3 (Mar 1926): 357–63.
‡ Rev. C. C. Colton, *Lacon* (1820) (William Gowans, 1855), 250 – though this may be much less true nowadays than it was then.
⊛ "Illness makes us disinclined for the long campaigns that prose exacts." Virginia Woolf, "On Being Ill" (1926), in *Selected Essays*, ed. David Bradshaw (Oxford University Press, 2008), 107.
¤ "Prolonged illness also carries the hazard of narcissistic self-absorption." Richard Hofstadter, *The American Political Tradition and the Men Who Made It* (1948) (Vintage, 1989), 420.

Erosrausch

eh-rohss-raussh

~

The head-over-heels intoxication of new love.

EROS-ECSTASY

Siechtumsschulung

zeecch-tooms – shoo-loong

~

The educative effects of serious illness.

INFIRMITY-INSTRUCTION

Schubladenbrief

shoob-lah-den – brief

~

The letter you write, but never send.

(DESK-)DRAWER-LETTER

Schottenfreude

112 The insight that entertainment is manufactured to be manipulative seems neither to negate its effect nor to diminish its popularity. In *c*.1944, Max Horkheimer and Theodor Adorno named such manufacture the "culture industry" (*Kulturindustrie*);[†] a few years later, George Orwell dubbed its product "prolefeed":

> Here were produced rubbishy newspapers, containing almost nothing except sport, crime, and astrology, sensational five-cent novelettes, films oozing with sex, and sentimental songs which were composed entirely by mechanical means on a special kind of kaleidoscope known as a versificator.[‡]

† See Max Horkheimer & Theodor W. Adorno, *Dialektik der Aufklärung* [*Dialectic of Enlightenment*] (Querido, 1947).
‡ George Orwell, *Nineteen Eighty-Four* (1949) (Signet, 1977), 43.
» Noël Coward's line "Extraordinary how potent cheap music is"* is curious, since he was "born into a generation that still took light music seriously,"[§] and wrote classics of that genre. * Noël Coward, *Private Lives*, 1930, A i; § Hoare, *Noël Coward*, op. cit., 12.
➤ *Schlager* music is camp, sentimental, and inexplicably popular.

113 This encapsulates a range of anxieties, for example:

> Paranoia on going through customs, even though you are carrying no contraband.

> Decelerating as you drive past a police car.

> Answering those in authority with vastly more information than they require.[†]

> Making an elaborate show of holding an item as you walk into a store, so as not to be accused of shoplifting.

> Fearing that an unexpected official-looking letter contains bad news.

† In German: *vorauseilender Gehorsam* ("anticipatory obedience").
» "The more virtuous a man is, the more severe and distrustful is [his conscience's] behaviour, so that ultimately it is precisely those people who have carried saintliness furthest who reproach themselves with the worst sinfulness." Freud, *Civilization and Its Discontents*, op. cit., 87.

114 Charles Dickens neatly illustrated how marginal the collapse from solvency to debt can be:

> Annual income twenty pounds, annual expenditure nineteen nineteen six, result happiness. Annual income twenty pounds, annual expenditure twenty pounds ought and six, result misery. The blossom is blighted, the leaf is withered, the God of day goes down upon the dreary scene, and – and in short you are for ever floored.[†]

François Rabelais gave Panurge a contrary viewpoint:

> God forbid that I should be debt-free. … Always owe something to someone. Then there will be prayers continually offered up to God to grant you a long and happy life.[‡]

† Charles Dickens, *The Personal History of David Copperfield* (Bradbury & Evans, 1850), 125–26.
‡ François Rabelais, *Gargantua and Pantagruel* (1532–?64), trans. J. M. Cohen (Penguin, 1955), 295.

112 — Schlagerschmeichelei

shlah-gher – shmycch-eh-lie

Enjoying emotionally manipulative mass culture, despite knowing you are being manipulated.

SCHLAGER-INGRATIATION

113 — Amtsangst

ahmts-ahngst

Irrational feelings of guilt suffered by the spotlessly innocent.

AUTHORITY-ANXIETY

114 — Damoklesschuld

dah-mo-cles – shoold

The haunting anxiety of owing money you cannot pay back.

DAMOCLES-DEBT

115 Such pride is what economists term a "wasting asset," since any uniqueness you feel at being about in the early hours will gradually fade as others wake up. ❦ Founded in 1084 by Saint Bruno of Cologne, the Order of Carthusians places great emphasis on being awake while others are asleep. Monks of this austere and severe order gather each night, between 11 P.M. and 2 A.M., to chant psalms in Latin and read scripture.

> The tradition, started in the fifteenth century, of getting up in the middle of the night, of being on duty, on call, keeping watch, harmonized with the life. The monks keep vigil like the shepherds in Bethlehem. … The Carthusians prize this time as their signature contribution to other men.[†]

---

† Nancy Klein Maguire, *An Infinity of Little Hours: Five Young Men and Their Trial of Faith in the Western World's Most Austere Monastic Order* (PublicAffairs, 2006), 31. Carthusian monks are both *cenobitic* (community-living) and *eremitic* (solitary).
» Similar is the pleasure of being awake before the alarm goes off.
↝ *Früh* ("early"); *Fröhlichkeit* ("happiness" or "gaiety").

116 Being forced to divert a conversation having lost your train of thought is deeply aggravating – and it creates an unease similar to that of *Zeigarnikfrustration* (☞59). Thomas Hobbes explored the mind's ability to track back and forth to reacquire what has been lost, in a passage titled "Of the Consequence or Trayne of Imaginations":

> Sometimes a man seeks what he hath lost; and from that place, and time, wherein he misses it, his mind runs back, from place to place, and time to time, to find where, and when he had it; that is to say, to find some certain, and limited time and place, in which to begin a method of seeking. Again, from thence, his thoughts run over the same places and times, to find what action, or other occasion might make him lose it.[†]

---

† Thomas Hobbes, *Leviathan: Or the Matter, Forme & Power of a Commonwealth, Ecclesiasticall and Civill* (1651), ed. A. R. Waller (Cambridge University Press, 1904), 10.

117 Adults routinely deceive children, by perpetuating myths ("Father Christmas comes only if you are asleep"); deploying sleight of hand (losing a game, without being caught); and telling lies ("The jingle means the van's run out of ice cream"). Socrates argued there were times when lies were justified, for example, tricking a child into taking medicine.[†] Jean-Jacques Rousseau, however, gave the following admonition:

> One cannot teach children the danger of lying to men without being aware of the greater danger, on the part of men, of lying to children. A single proved lie told by the master to the child would ruin forever the whole fruit of the education.[‡]

---

† Xenophon, *Memorabilia of Sokrates*, bk 4, ch. 2, § 17, trans. George B. Wheeler (William Allan, 1847), 167.
‡ Jean-Jacques Rousseau, *Emile: Or On Education* (1762), trans. & ed. C. Kelly & A. Bloom (Dartmouth College Press, 2010), 367.
» For a crowd-sourced view of lies told to children, see "Schott's Vocab" (blog), *The New York Times*, 12 xi 2010, nyti.ms/9yOd8p.

Fröhlichkeit

fruu-licch-kite

~

Feeling uniquely ſpecial at being up and about while others are ſtill abed.

EARLY-GAIETY

Ideenentgleisung

ee-deh-en – ent-gly-zoong

~

Irritation at losing one's train of thought.

IDEA-DERAILMENT

Kinderhalbwahrheit

kin-der – hahlb-vahr-hite

~

The myriad deceptions adults practiſe on children.

CHILDREN-HALF-TRUTH

118 A clinical diagnosis of Obsessive-Compulsive Disorder usually requires that the symptoms cause real distress and significantly impair normal routines and relationships.[†] However, many experience "OCD lite" symptoms, which are often more curious than onerous. Some symptoms are exaggerations of common sense, or manifestations of slenderly held superstitions; others seem to be spillovers from "attention to detail" that is functional in other aspects of life. For example:

(Re)checking the iron/stove/oven/water is off. ❦ (Re)checking the alarm is on. ❦ (Re)checking the front door is locked, having just left the house or just settled in bed. ❦ Counting steps or stairs. ❦ Touching railings. ❦ Flushing a toilet (or lifting the seat) with your foot. (☞89) ❦ Avoiding pavement cracks. ❦ Returning to the same toilet stall or urinal. ❦ (Un)dressing in a specific order. ❦ Planning your final mouthful of food. ❦ Re-washing your hands.[‡] ❦ Setting alarms to an odd/even/lucky time. (☞37) ❦ Setting multiple alarms. ❦ Setting your watch fast. ❦ (Re)checking your phone is off, even by turning it on and off again. ❦ (Re)checking your earrings, or that the stone is still in your engagement ring. ❦ (Re)checking the right letter is in the right envelope.[*]

† See, for example, *Diagnostic and Statistical Manual of Mental Disorders*, 4th ed. Text Rev. (American Psychiatric Assoc., 2000), 300·3.
‡ See William Shakespeare, *Macbeth*, c.1606, A v, S i, ll. 26–52.
* Yet G. K. Chesterton wrote, "A man might actually succeed in journalism by writing articles exactly appropriate to all the journals, and then putting them all into the wrong envelopes." "Succeeding in Journalism," *Illustrated London News*, 21 viii 1909.
↜ *Neuröschen* means both "little neurosis" and "little new roses."

⁎   ⁎   ⁎

119 The ambivalence of some prayers was deftly described by the writer Sarah Lyall in a diary entry about her husband, Robert McCrum, who was at the time recovering after a stroke:

> I pray to a God I don't believe in. But I had an absurd thought the other day, that the thing about God is that even if you don't believe in him, he listens to you. Maybe there's some religion in me after all.[†]

† Robert McCrum, *My Year Off* (W. W. Norton, 1998), 114.

120 Johann Wolfgang von Goethe conveyed this unique pleasure with poetic elegance:

> And first his head upon cool pillow lay,
> Then bathe ye him in dew from Lethe's stream;
> His limbs, cramp-stiffen'd, will more freely play,
> If sleep-refreshed he wait morn's wakening beam.[†]

Marcel Proust added:

> I laid my cheek against the pillow's blooming cheeks, which, forever plump and cool, are like the cheeks of our childhood against which we press our own.[‡]

And Emily Holt agreed: "Nothing so rests a tired or fevered head as a fresh, cool pillow."[*]

† Johann Wolfgang von Goethe, *The Tragedy of Faust*, pt II, A I (1832), in *Goethe's Faust*, trans. Anna Swanwick (G. Bell, 1905), 171.
‡ *Marcel Proust: On Art and Literature 1896–1919*, trans. Sylvia Townsend Warner (1954) (Carroll & Graf, 1997), 27.
* Emily Holt, *The Complete Housekeeper* (Doubleday, 1917), 336.

Neuröschen

noy-roos-sh'yen

~

Everyday quirks of quasi-obsessive and sub-compulsive behaviour.

LITTLE-NEUROSES

Götzengeschwätz

goot-sen – ghe-shvetz

~

Praying to a god you don't believe in.

IDOL-CHATTER

Kissenkühlelabsal

kis-sen – kuu-leh – lahb-zahl

~

The ineffable pleasure, and instant relief, of a cool pillow.

PILLOW-CHILL-REFRESHMENT

Schottenfreude

Index

Schottenfreude

Schottenfreude™

GERMAN WORDS FOR THE HUMAN CONDITION

A CIP catalogue record for this title is available from the British Library.

ISBN 978-1-84854-910-4

Printed and bound in China

First published in Great Britain in 2013 by

JOHN MURRAY (Publishers)

An Hachette UK Company

© BEN SCHOTT 2013

www.benschott.com · Twitter: @benschott

2

John Murray policy is to use papers that are natural, renewable and recyclable products and made from wood grown in sustainable forests. The logging and manufacturing processes are expected to conform to the environmental regulations of the country of origin.

John Murray (Publishers)
50 Victoria Embankment, London, EC4Y 0DZ
www.johnmurray.co.uk

A NOTE ON THE TYPE · The blackletter font is Journalistic, designed by Andrew Leman; the body text is Adobe's Garamond Premier Pro. Certain conventions of traditional German orthography have been relaxed for ease of reading.

"These things are not words, they are alphabetical processions."

Mark Twain, "The Awful German Language,"
in *A Tramp Abroad*, vol. 2, app. D (Chatto & Windus, 1880), 277